BECAUSE VIOLENCE CAN ONLY BREED
MORE VIOLENCE AND SUFFERING,
OUR STRUGGLE MUST REMAIN NON-VIOLENT
AND FREE OF HATRED.

HIS HOLINESS
THE 14TH DALAI LAMA

BioGraphic Novel: The 14th Dalai Lama
A graphic adaptation of the true story about
his country, his people, his struggle, and his non-violence

By Tetsu Saiwai

EMOTIONAL
CONTENT

BioGraphic Novel is a series of mangas
(graphic novels or comic books) that portray
the lives of historical figures who changed the world.
You can find additional information regarding
other biographic novel projects at:

http://www.biographicnovel.com

Published by:

Emotional Content LLC.
P.O. Box 251863
Los Angeles, CA 90025
Email: info@biographicnovel.com
Web: http://www.emotionalcontent.net

Printed in the United States of America
Cover photo by Stephan Bollinger
Copyright © 2008 swissphoto australia
Also supplied from Tibet Religious Foundation of His Holiness the Dalai Lama

ISBN: 978-0-9817543-0-7 Paperback
Library of Congress Control Number: 2008930271

1.0

DEDICATION

This book is dedicated to those who lost their lives in
Tibet under the Chinese invasion over the last half-century .

We believe it is our responsibility not only to learn what
happened, but to educate and empower the next generation so they
may ensure the same mistakes are not repeated anywhere else
in the world.

May all their precious souls, both Tibetan and Chinese,
rest in peace.

A GRAPHIC ADAPTATION
OF THE TRUE STORY
ABOUT HIS COUNTRY,
HIS PEOPLE,
HIS STRUGGLE,
AND HIS NON-VIOLENCE

BioGraphic Novel : Series 1

The 14th
Dalai Lama

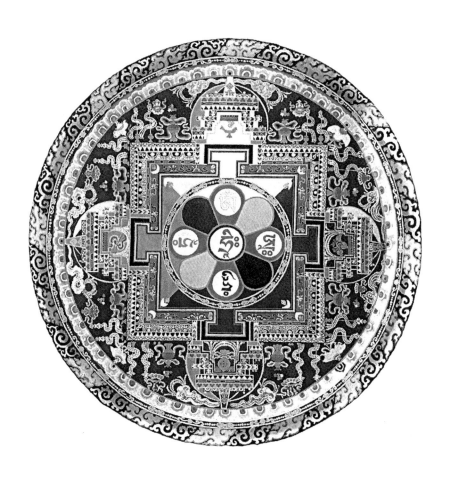

Tetsu Saiwai

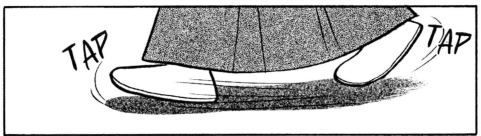

WHAT CAN I DO FOR YOU, *RETING RINPOCHE?*

I RECEIVED A MESSAGE.

I SAW A VISION OF THE 3 TIBETAN LETTERS "AH, KA, MA" ON THE SURFACE OF THE WATER DURING MY TRIP TO THE SACRED LAKE *LHAMO LHATSO*.

I ALSO SAW IMAGES OF A THREE-STOREYED MONASTERY WITH A GOLD AND TURQUOISE ROOF...

AND A PATH LEADING UP A HILL.

THE IMAGE OF A SMALL HOUSE WITH A STRANGELY SHAPED ROOF CAUGHT MY EYE, AS WELL.

THAT IS WHERE THE 14TH REINCARNATED DALAI LAMA AWAITS US.

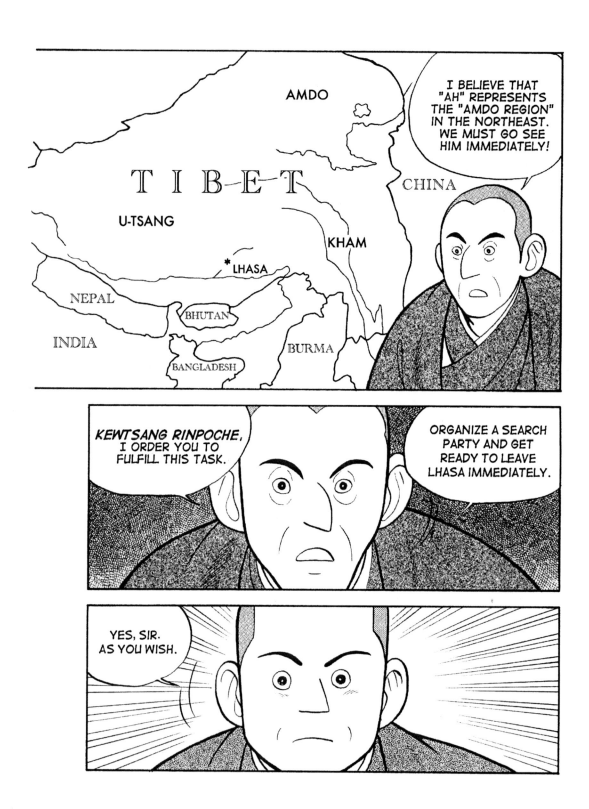

"DALAI" MEANS "BIG OCEAN" IN MONGOLIAN.

"LAMA" MEANS "TEACHER" IN TIBETAN, JUST AS "GURU" DOES IN THE HINDU LANGUAGE.

THE PHRASE "DALAI LAMA" MEANS "THE SPIRITUAL LEADER OF TIBET."

OUR COUNTRY HAS BEEN GOVERNED BY 13 DALAI LAMAS WHO ARE BELIEVED TO BE THE REINCARNATION OF BUDDHA.

BUT THE DALAI LAMAS DO NOT RULE AS A FAMILY DYNASTY. INSTEAD, WE BELIEVE THAT WHEN THE BODY OF THE DALAI LAMA DIES, HIS SOUL IS REBORN AS A CHILD WHO WILL SUCCEED HIM.

IT WAS 1939 WHEN THE SEARCH MISSION FOUND ME TO BE THE REINCARNATION OF THE 13TH DALAI LAMA.

I WAS JUST TWO YEARS OLD...

AMDO PROVINCE, KUMBUM MONASTERY

HMMM, THIS MUST BE THE MONASTERY HE WAS TALKING ABOUT...

I SEE A PATH LEADING UP A HILL...

AND, ACCORDING TO THE MESSAGE, WE SHOULD FIND A HOUSE WITH A STRANGELY SHAPED ROOF.

OH! THIS MUST BE IT...

WAIT A MINUTE...

PLEASE TAKE THIS, AND GIVE IT TO YOUR KIDS ALSO!

OH, NO, IT IS TOO MUCH. YOU HAVE GIVEN US SO MUCH ALREADY...

NOT AT ALL! WE NEED TO HELP EACH OTHER OUT, ESPECIALLY DURING TOUGH TIMES...

THANK YOU SO MUCH FOR BEING SO KIND, EVEN THOUGH WE'VE JUST MET.

MOM, ARE THEY CHINESE?

YES, THEY CROSSED THE BORDER TO GET SOME FOOD.

YOU SEE, *LLHAMO*, THERE ARE NO BOUNDARIES WHEN IT COMES TO CARING FOR EACH OTHER. WE'RE ALL HERE TO HELP EACH OTHER.

YOU CAN USE THIS ROOM.

THANK YOU VERY MUCH.

WELL, GOOD EVENING!

WHAT IS YOUR NAME, YOUNG MAN?

MY NAME IS LLHAMO.

I SEE. I AM A SERVANT OF THAT GENTLEMAN...

NO, YOU'RE NOT! YOU'RE SERA LAMA (A NOBLE MONK AT THE SERA MONASTERY).

LLHAMO DÖNDRUB 2 YEARS OLD

LLHAMO! LUNCH IS READY!

THAT'S MY SEAT, DAD! LET ME SIT THERE!

OH MY! HERE WE GO AGAIN... YOU SAY THAT!

LLHAMO, THE SEAT AT THAT END BELONGS TO THE HEAD OF THE FAMILY.

NO! THIS IS MY SEAT!

HA HA HA! YOU ARE SO STUBBORN!

LISTEN, NOW... IF YOU SIT AT THE END OF THE TABLE, YOU HAVE TO BEAR A LOT OF RESPONSIBILITY!

I KNOW!

I WONDER WHAT HE KNOWS...

IN RETROSPECT, I MAY HAVE KNOWN WHAT MY MISSIONS WERE...

NEIGH

OK, I'M OFF TO THE TOWN OF SILIN TODAY.

TAKE CARE OF YOURSELF. OH, BY THE WAY, WOULD YOU BRING BACK SOME SUGAR?

NO PROBLEM! WE SEEM TO HAVE A GOOD HARVEST THIS YEAR!!

WE CAN TRADE OUR CROPS FOR SUGAR, COTTON TEXTILES... EVEN A HORSE!

HEY, LITTLE MAN! WHERE DO YOU THINK YOU'RE GOING WITH THOSE BAGS?

I'M GOING TO LHASA!

SERA LAMA!

WHICH ONES ARE YOURS?

......

THIS IS MINE!

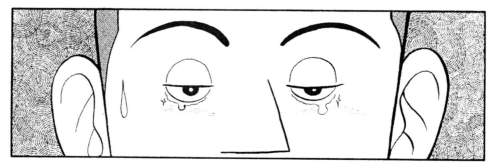

THAT'S RIGHT. THE ONES YOU HAVE CHOSEN REALLY DO BELONG TO YOU...

THE 13TH DALAI LAMA USED THEM... YOU...

WELCOME BACK, YOUR HOLINESS...

THE 14TH DALAI LAMA!

SUMMER 1939

BROTHER *THUBTEN*! WHAT'S GOING TO HAPPEN NOW? AND WHO IS THE DALAI LAMA?

.....

ONE WHO COMES BACK TO THIS WORLD TO SAVE THE LIVES OF ALL LIVING CREATURES...

YOU HAVE TREMENDOUS RESPONSIBILITIES NOW, AND THIS, THIS IS YOUR DESTINY...

THUBTEN JIGME NORBU (TAKSTER RINPOCHE) ELDEST BROTHER

DALAI LAMA, 5 YEARS OLD

ALL RIGHT THEN, IT'S TIME TO MOVE OUT TO LHASA!

BROTHER, REST ASSURED THAT I'LL TAKE GOOD CARE OF HIM!

I'M COUNTING ON YOU, *LOBSANG SAMTEN.*

FATHER, MOTHER. SAFE JOURNEY!

MY THOUGHTS ARE WITH YOU!

LOOK AT THE HERD OF DRONGS!! (WILD YAKS)

WOW, BEAUTIFUL TIBETAN SEROWS!

PLEASE MEET HIS HOLINESS...

YOUR HOLINESS! THANK YOU FOR COMING ALL THIS WAY. HOW NICE IT IS TO HAVE YOU BACK!

I'M THE REGENT, RETING RINPOCHE.

BEFORE WE GO INTO LHASA, WHICH IS NOT VERY FAR FROM HERE, WE WILL NEED TO CONDUCT A SPECIAL CEREMONY.

THE CEREMONY IS A RITUAL THAT OFFICIALLY ACKNOWLEDGES YOU AS THE SPIRITUAL LEADER OF TIBET.

THE RITUAL WAS HELD IN DOCTAN, THREE KILOMETERS AWAY FROM THE GATES TO THE CAPITAL CITY OF LHASA. I WAS OFFICIALLY RECOGNIZED AS THE REINCARNATED DALAI LAMA AND RENAMED *JETSUN JAMPHEL NGAWANG LOBSANG YESHE TENZIN GYATSO.* ("HOLY LORD, GENTLE GLORY, COMPASSIONATE, DEFENDER OF THE FAITH, OCEAN OF WISDOM")

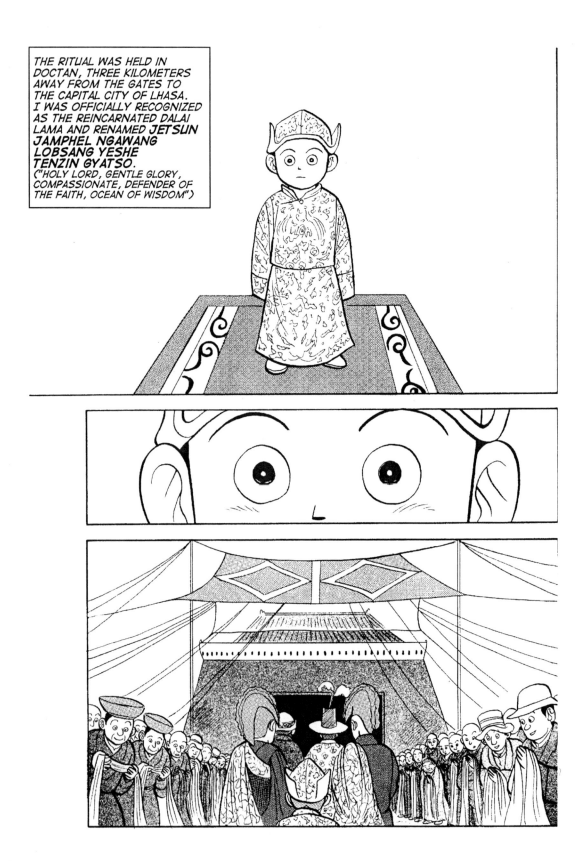

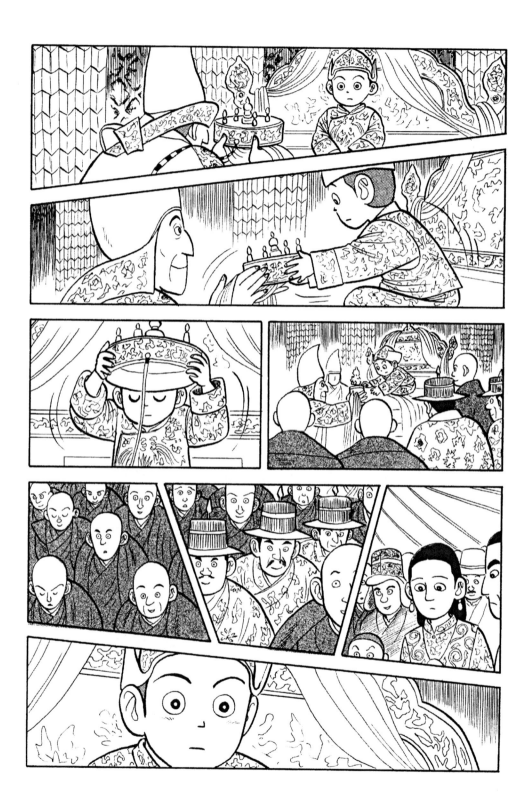

WINTER 1939,
THE DALAI LAMA ARRIVES IN LHASA

YOUR HOLINESS.
THIS IS THE GATE TO
LHASA, BANGORILKAN.
ONCE YOU WALK THROUGH
IT, YOU ARE IN LHASA.

THIS IS
THE *NORBULINGKA*
PALACE.

YOU WILL SPEND THE NEXT YEAR HERE, UNTIL THE OFFICIAL ENTHRONEMENT CEREMONY AT THE *POTALA* PALACE.

... BUT WHAT ABOUT MY MOM AND DAD?!

DON'T WORRY. THEY'LL STAY HERE WITH YOU.

YOUR PARENTS HAVE A SEPARATE AREA TO STAY INSIDE THE PALACE.

THEY WILL SURELY BECOME THE MOST NOBLE ARISTOCRATS!

IN RETROSPECT, I THINK THIS MAY HAVE BEEN THE HAPPIEST PERIOD IN MY LIFE.

IN THE WINTER OF 1940, I HAD TO MOVE FROM THE NORBULINGKA PALACE TO THE POTALA PALACE.

IT WAS AT THIS TIME THAT I FORMALLY ASCENDED THE THRONE OF TIBET AS ITS SPIRITUAL LEADER AT THE **SI SHI PHUNTSOG** (HALL OF ALL GOOD DEEDS OF THE SPIRITUAL AND TEMPORAL WORLD).

WHERE IS MY MOM?

WHAT ABOUT MY DAD?

CAN LOBSANG STAY WITH ME?

THE THRONE THAT YOU SAT ON EARLIER AT SI SHI PHUNTSOG IS CALLED THE "LION THRONE."

THAT IS WHERE ONLY THE TRUE SPIRITUAL LEADER OF TIBET CAN SIT.

YOU WILL START YOUR NEW LIFE AS THE 14TH DALAI LAMA AT THE POTALA PALACE.

WHILE YOU RECEIVE YOUR TRAINING IN RELIGIOUS AUSTERITY UNTIL 18 YEARS OF AGE,

I WILL CONTINUE LEADING THE POLITICS AS THE REGENT ON YOUR BEHALF.

IN THE MEANTIME, PLEASE ALLOW ME TO BE YOUR MENTOR, OR PERHAPS YOUR PRIVATE TUTOR...

IN ADDITION, *TATHAG RINPOCHE* WILL BE YOUR LOWER-LEVEL PRIVATE TUTOR, AND KEWTSANG RINPOCHE WILL BE YOUR UNOFFICIAL PRIVATE TUTOR.

I WILL BE CONDUCTING LECTURES ON THE RECITATION OF THE HOLY SCRIPTS.

MUMBLE MUMBLE

YOUR HOLINESS! PLEASE RECITE USING A STRONG, CLEAR VOICE!

I AM IN CHARGE OF THE READING AND WRITING CLASSES...

AND YOU SHOULD KNOW NOW THAT I WILL BE STRICT!

YOU SEE THE SILK WHIP AND LEATHER WHIP BACK THERE?!

THE SILK ONE IS FOR HIS HOLINESS, AND THE LEATHER ONE IS FOR LOBSANG. STUDY HARD OR YOU WILL NOT ONLY HEAR THE CRACK OF THE WHIP, BUT YOU WILL FEEL IT, TOO!

YOU UNDERSTAND, RIGHT? YOU MUST DO YOUR BEST!!

READING AND WRITING WILL GIVE YOU A SOLID FOUNDATION FOR THE STUDIES OF PHILOSOPHY, HISTORY, GRAMMAR, AND MEDICINE, ALL OF WHICH YOU WILL TAKE UP LATER.

MOM...

ARE YOU STILL AWAKE, *KUNDUN*? (AN AFFECTIONATE NICKNAME FOR THE DALAI LAMA)

PONPO! I MISS MY MOM! WHY DO I HAVE TO GO THROUGH THIS?!

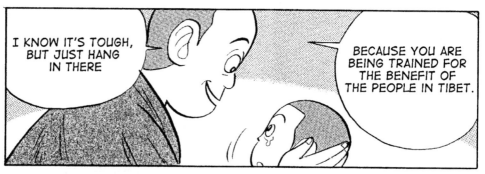

I KNOW IT'S TOUGH, BUT JUST HANG IN THERE

BECAUSE YOU ARE BEING TRAINED FOR THE BENEFIT OF THE PEOPLE IN TIBET.

WHAT DO YOU MEAN?

YOU ARE LEARNING FOR US THE WAYS IN WHICH PEOPLE CAN BE HAPPY.

PLEASE WIN THE HEARTS AND MINDS OF THE TIBETAN PEOPLE, AND THEN TEACH US WHAT GENUINE HAPPINESS REALLY IS.

EVERY PERSON WANTS TO HAVE A HAPPY LIFE.

KUNDUN, TIBET IS FULL OF PEOPLE WHO NEVER HAVE A CHANCE TO RECEIVE A PROPER EDUCATION BECAUSE THEY ARE SO POOR.

I KNOW THIS BECAUSE I USED TO BE ONE OF THEM.

PLEASE KEEP THAT IN MIND.

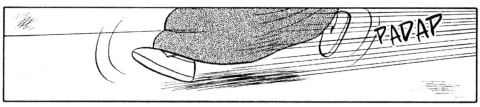

PADAP

GOOD MORNING, PONPO! I WANT PORK FOR LUNCH TODAY!

YOU KNOW THAT A NOVICE MONK IS PROHIBITED FROM EATING MEAT!

JUST KIDDING!

SOON AFTERWARD, SOMETHING SAD HAPPENED. RETING RINPOCHE, WHO DISCOVERED ME, RESIGNED HIS POSITION AS REGENT. HE ALSO RESIGNED AS MY PRIVATE TUTOR.

!

RETING RINPOCHE HAS RESIGNED? AND HE'S NOT MY TUTOR ANYMORE, EITHER?!

WHAT'S GOING ON?!

I'M SORRY, BUT I HAVE NO ANSWERS FOR YOU.

WE HAVE NO REGENT LEADING THE CONGRESS NOW. IT FALLS TO YOU TO APPOINT A NEW REGENT.

OK, TATHAG RINPOCHE, I APPOINT YOU TO THE POSITION!

!

AS YOU WISH. I WILL SERVE AS REGENT FROM HERE ON IN.

HIS HOLINESS HAS APPOINTED ME TO BE THE REGENT FROM TODAY ON, AND I WILL LEAD THE CONGRESS.

IN THIS WAY, THE TIBETAN GOVERNMENT RECEIVED TATHAG RINPOCHE AS ITS NEW POLITICAL LEADER.

1. ABOVE
Lhamo Lhatso,
the Sacred Lake

2. LEFT
H.H. The Dalai Lama
as a child

Source:
Tibet Religious Foundation
of His Holiness the Dalai Lama

3. ABOVE
H.H. The Dalai Lama on his Throne
at the Potala Palace

4. LEFT
H.H. The Dalai Lama as a teenager

Source:
Tibet Religious Foundation of
His Holiness the Dalai Lama

IT TOOK A WHILE BEFORE I LEARNED THAT RETING RINPOCHE HAD GONE INTO POLITICS FOR HIS OWN BENEFIT. HE DISAPPOINTED THE TIBETAN PEOPLE BY BREAKING HIS VOW OF CELIBACY.

SIX YEARS AFTER RETING RINPOCHE LEFT POLITICS,

A UNFORSEEN SHAMEFUL EVENT OCCURRED...

EARLY SPRING IN 1947

YOUR HOLINESS, PLEASE DEFINE THE MEANING OF "ENLIGHTENMENT"

WELL..., ENLIGHTENMENT IS... UMM...

DALAI LAMA 12 YEARS OLD

YOUR HOLINESS! PLEASE LOOK ME IN THE EYE WHEN YOU ANSWER!

I'M SORRY...

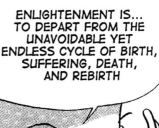

ENLIGHTENMENT IS... TO DEPART FROM THE UNAVOIDABLE YET ENDLESS CYCLE OF BIRTH, SUFFERING, DEATH, AND REBIRTH

AND TO ELIMINATE KARMA AND ALL THE NEGATIVE DEEDS, INCLUDING TEMPORAL OBSESSION.

THAT IS CORRECT.

PANG PANG

YOUR HOLINESS, SEEK SHELTER IMMEDIATELY!

WHAT.. WHAT HAPPENED?

GUNSHOTS WERE HEARD FROM THE SERA MONASTERY! THERE IS SHOOTING AT THE RETING MONASTERY, AS WELL! PEOPLE HAVE BEEN KILLED!

WHAT!? WHAT IS GOING ON?

RETING RINPOCHE ATTACKED TATHAG RINPOCHE, TRYING TO REGAIN POLITICAL POWER!!

WHY ON EARTH...!? IS TATHAG RINPOCHE ALL RIGHT!?

PANG PANG PANG

PANG PANG PANG PANG

WHAT HAPPENED WAS A TRAGEDY...

... INVOLVING THE ATTEMPTED MURDER OF A MONK BY ANOTHER MONK WHO PREACHED ABOUT THE VIRTUES OF "ENLIGHTENMENT."

A NUMBER OF PEOPLE WERE INJURED OR LOST THEIR LIVES, WHILE THE RETING MONASTERY, ONE OF THE OLDEST AND MOST BEAUTIFUL MONASTERIES IN TIBET, WAS DESTROYED.

WHAT WILL HAPPEN TO RETING RINPOCHE?

AFTER BEING HELD IN PRISON, HE WILL BE PUT ON TRIAL.

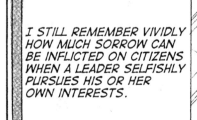

I STILL REMEMBER VIVIDLY HOW MUCH SORROW CAN BE INFLICTED ON CITIZENS WHEN A LEADER SELFISHLY PURSUES HIS OR HER OWN INTERESTS.

I WAS NOT ALLOWED TO PLAY OUTSIDE, SO I USED TO LOOK ON ENVIOUSLY AS OTHER CHILDREN PLAYED IN THE COURTYARD.

SHFFF

SHFFFF

IT'S A HUMBLE, BUT A PEACEFUL LIFE...

I AM EMBARRASSED TO HAVE WITNESSED SUCH AN UGLY POLITICAL POWER STRUGGLE THE OTHER DAY.

YOUR HOLINESS! MR. *HEINRICH HARRER* IS HERE TO SEE YOU!

OH, REALLY!?

HE'S ONE OF THE MOST WELL-KNOWN MOUNTAIN CLIMBERS IN AUSTRIA!

I CAN'T WAIT TO HEAR ABOUT HIS ADVENTURES, AND HOW HE ESCAPED FROM THE BRITISH CONCENTRATION CAMP IN INDIA TO REACH LHASA DURING WORLD WAR II.

IT IS SUCH AN HONOR TO MEET YOU, YOUR HOLINESS.

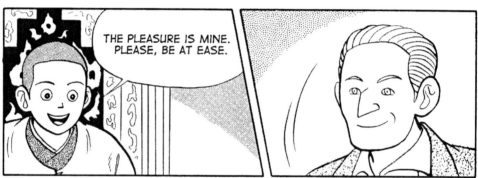

THE PLEASURE IS MINE. PLEASE, BE AT EASE.

THANK YOU FOR COMING. WOULD YOU BE WILLING TO TEACH ME ABOUT EUROPE? I WANT TO KNOW WHAT IT'S LIKE OUTSIDE TIBET.

CERTAINLY! IT WOULD BE MY PLEASURE!

GREAT! THERE IS SO MUCH I AM CURIOUS ABOUT!

THANK YOU FOR FIXING THE GENERATOR. IF YOU HADN'T DONE IT, WE COULDN'T HAVE USED THIS PROJECTOR.

YOUR HOLINESS, AS YOU CAN SEE IN THESE NEWSREELS, MANY LIVES WERE LOST DURING WORLD WAR II. UNFORTUNATELY, TREMENDOUS MISERY AND SORROW GO HAND IN HAND WITH WAR...

EVEN NUCLEAR WEAPONS WERE USED. TWO ATOMIC BOMBS WERE DROPPED ON JAPAN...

HUMAN BEINGS HAVE CREATED HELL ON THIS PRECIOUS EARTH...

WHAT ARE YOU DOING THIS LATE IN THE EVENING?

LISTEN, PONPO...

YES, KUNDUN?

WHY DOES WAR OCCUR? WHY DO PEOPLE HAVE TO KILL EACH OTHER?

WAR OFTEN BREAKS OUT WHEN ONE COUNTRY INVADES ANOTHER FOR ITS OWN SELFISH GAIN. MANY, MANY PEOPLE ARE KILLED IN THE PROCESS.

AND IT IS SO OFTEN INNOCENT CIVILIANS WHO PAY THE PRICE, LOSING THEIR LIVES. MOST OFTEN, THE HARDEST-HIT ARE CHILDREN, WOMEN, AND OLD PEOPLE...

TIBET IS A BUDDHIST NATION, AND KEPT A NEUTRAL STANCE EVEN DURING WORLD WAR II. WE HAVE NEITHER INVADED OTHER NATIONS NOR GIVEN A HAND TO INVADERS.

HOWEVER, TIBET HAS ALWAYS BEEN A TARGET FOR INVASION FROM OTHER COUNTRIES.

BOTH BRITAIN AND THE *QING DYNASTY* (CHINA) TRIED TO OCCUPY TIBET DURING THE RULE OF THE LAST DALAI LAMA.

AND NOW, WE SENSE THAT CHINA IS PLANNING SOMETHING ONCE AGAIN.

KUNDUN, PLEASE KEEP A CLOSE EYE ON CHINA'S MOVEMENTS.

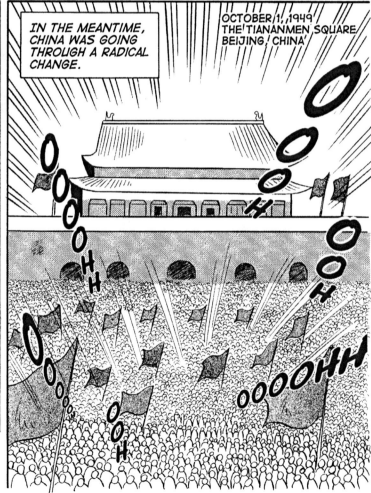

IN THE MEANTIME, CHINA WAS GOING THROUGH A RADICAL CHANGE.

OCTOBER 1, 1949 THE TIANANMEN SQUARE BEIJING, CHINA

I HEREBY DECLARE THE BEGINNING OF **THE PEOPLE'S REPUBLIC OF CHINA!**

LED BY CHAIRMAN **MAO ZEDONG,** COMMUNISM OVERTOOK CHINA.

WE ARE PLEASED TO INFORM YOU THAT, AFTER A 20-YEAR CIVIL WAR, OUR GREAT NATION...

... REBORN AS THE PEOPLE'S REPUBLIC OF CHINA. OUR GREAT LEADER, CHAIRMAN MAO, IS...

KUNDUN... THIS IS SOMETHING OF GREAT SIGNIFICANCE TO US...

WHAT DO YOU MEAN?

I AM WORRIED ABOUT WHAT THE NEWLY UNITED CHINA WILL DEMAND OF OUR NATION UNDER THE COMMUNIST PARTY...

BEFORE LONG, PONPO'S FEARS CAME TRUE... WE HEARD UNBELIEVABLE CLAIMS FROM A BEIJING-BASED RADIO STATION.

"TIBET IS JUST A PART OF THE PEOPLE'S REPUBLIC OF CHINA..."

THE LIBERATION ARMY WILL MARCH ON AND EMANCIPATE ITS TIBETAN PEOPLE FROM THE HANDS OF THE FOREIGN IMPERIALISTS!

THE TIBETAN GOVERNMENT IMMEDIATELY LAUNCHED AN OFFICIAL DEMONSTRATION AGAINST THE CHINESE GOVERNMENT AND ISSUED A PRESS RELEASE.

TIBET HAS NEVER BEEN A PART OF CHINA, AND THERE ARE NO IMPERIALISTS OCCUPYING OUR NATION, AS CHINA CLAIMS! THEREFORE, WE DO NOT HAVE ANY NEED AT ALL FOR EMANCIPATION!

HOWEVER...

RRRRHUUUMMM

THE CHINESE LIBERATION ARMY HAS ALREADY GATHERED ITS TROOPS AT THE BORDER FACING THE EASTERN PART OF TIBET. THEY MAY ADVANCE AT ANY MOMENT.

FACING AN IMMINENT CRISIS, THE TIBETAN CONGRESS CALLED AN EMERGENCY ASSEMBLY.

WE MUST GET SOME SUPPORT FROM *ENGLAND, AMERICA, INDIA* OR EVEN *NEPAL* BEFORE IT'S TOO LATE!

THERE IS NO WAY THAT OUR ARMY ALONE CAN PROTECT US AGAINST THE CHINESE, WHO HAVE SEVERAL MILLION SOLDIERS!

THERE ARE NO OTHER OPTIONS...

WE WILL DISPATCH A PETITION TO EACH OF THE FOUR COUNTRIES, ASKING THEM FOR ADVICE AS TO HOW WE CAN STOP CHINA FROM INVADING TIBET.

AGREED!

MISSIONS WERE ASSEMBLED AND DISPATCHED TO THOSE COUNTRIES IMMEDIATELY.

NEVERTHELESS...

YAAHHH

YAAAHHHH

YAAAHHHH

ON OCTOBER 7, 1950, THE CHINESE LIBERATION ARMY MADE A FULL-FLEDGED ATTACK ON THE CAPITAL OF EASTERN TIBET, CHAMDO.

KAPOW

TOGETHER WITH THE **KHAMPA RESISTANCE ARMY**, WHICH CONSISTED OF LOCAL VOLUNTEERS, THE TIBETAN BORDER POLICE FOUGHT BACK.

BLAAAAM

HOWEVER...

BRAAAAP

BRRRR

BRRRR

THE RESISTANCE WAS NO MATCH FOR THE OVERWHELMING NUMBER OF SOLDIERS IN THE CHINESE LIBERATION ARMY.

IT IS REPORTED THAT MORE THAN 80,000 CHINESE SOLDIERS CROSSED THE DRICHU RIVER IN THE EAST OF CHAMDO, AND HAVE LANDED IN TIBETAN TERRITORY.

SO, IS OUR ARMY READY? ARE WE SUFFICIENTLY PREPARED?

COMPARED TO THE CHINESE ARMY, WHICH IS EQUIPPED WITH STATE-OF-THE-ART WEAPONS, WE HAVE PRACTICALLY NOTHING... WE ARE SIMPLY NOT IN THE SAME LEAGUE AS COMMUNIST CHINA.

ARE THERE ANY ALTERNATIVES?

ALTHOUGH WE BROUGHT THE CASE TO THE ATTENTION OF THE UNITED NATIONS, WE HAVE NOT HEARD ANYTHING FROM THEM.

SO YOU'RE SAYING THAT THERE'S NOTHING WE CAN DO... WE JUST HAVE TO ACCEPT IT AND SIT BACK AND WATCH IT GET WORSE!?

IF WE CAN'T DO ANYTHING ABOUT IT, WE'RE BETTER OFF LETTING THE DALAI LAMA TAKE CHARGE OF THE REGIME.

"LET HIS HOLINESS ASSUME POLITICAL CONTROL!"

KUNDUN, NOTICES DEMANDING YOUR RULE HAVE BEEN POSTED UP ALL OVER THE CITY!

BUT, I AM ONLY 15...

I AM FAR TOO YOUNG TO CARRY THAT MUCH RESPONSIBILITY...

THE CONGRESS IS OF TWO MINDS ABOUT THIS DECISION. SOME ARE IN FAVOR OF YOUR LEADERSHIP, WHILE OTHERS BELIEVE YOU ARE STILL TOO YOUNG FOR THE ROLE.

YOUR HOLINESS, THE ORACLE SUGGESTS THAT YOU SHOULD TAKE CONTROL OF THE ADMINISTRATION... ALLOW ME TO PREPARE TO RESIGN FROM THE REGENCY.

.....

REST ASSURED THAT I WILL STAY BY YOUR SIDE AND REMAIN AS YOUR MAIN PRIVATE TUTOR.

YOU HAVE, WITHOUT A SHADOW OF A DOUBT, BECOME THE LEADER OF SIX MILLION TIBETANS WHO ARE NOW CONFRONTING ALL-OUT WAR WITH CHINA.

WHAT CAN I DO...?

IS IT POSSIBLE FOR ME... TO LEAD...?

BROTHER THUBTEN! WHAT'S GOING TO HAPPEN NOW? AND WHO IS THE DALAI LAMA?

ONE WHO COMES BACK TO EARTH TO SAVE LIVES...

YOU HAVE TREMENDOUS RESPONSIBILITIES, AND THIS IS YOUR DESTINY...

BROTHER... I WONDER HOW YOU'RE DOING, AND WHAT OUR HOME, AMDO, LOOKS LIKE NOW...

KUNDUN!

THUD

BROTHER THUBTEN!!

DID YOU COME ALL THE WAY BACK FROM THE KUMBUM MONASTERY?

HOW ARE THINGS IN AMDO PROVINCE?

AMDO HAS BEEN ENTIRELY OCCUPIED BY THE CHINESE ARMY.

THE FIRST THING THEY TRIED TO DO UPON THEIR ARRIVAL WAS TO BAN OUR RELIGION.

THEY SAY THAT MONKS ARE NO LONGER PERMITTED TO ENGAGE IN THEIR RELIGIOUS DUTIES.

AS THE HEAD OF THE KUMBUM MONASTAERY, I WAS CONSTANTLY UNDER STRICT SURVEILLANCE.

THEY ALSO PREVENTED THE YOUTH FROM JOINING MONASTERIES, AND AS A RESULT, ARE ALL NOW COMPLETELY EMPTY.

MANY OF INFLUENTIAL LOCAL LEADERS WERE TAKEN TO A CONFERENCE IN BEIJING OR CHENGDU, AND FORCED TO RECEIVE A *"RE-EDUCATION."*

WHAT KIND OF EDUCATION IS IT, EXACTLY?

IT IS TO ACKNOWLEDGE THAT "TIBET IS A PART OF CHINA", AND WE SHOULD PRAISE COMMUNISM AND ITS PARTY LEADERS.

RECENTLY, EVEN CHILDREN ARE BEING SENT TO CHINA FOR THIS KIND OF RE-EDUCATION.

AND THE MOST ALARMING THING IS THAT THEY ARE BANNING THE USAGE OF THE TIBETAN LANGUAGE AND FORCING THE PEOPLE TO SPEAK CHINESE.

WHAT ON EARTH DO THEY MEAN BY EMANCIPATION!?

THEY'RE CHANGING THE WAY WE GROW OUR VEGETABLES AND CROPS, AND EVEN DICTATE TO US WHAT WE SHOULD GROW...

I REALLY BELIEVE THAT BEFORE WE KNOW IT, TIBETAN TRADITIONS AND IDENTITIES WILL BE LOST.

THE EMANCIPATION OF TIBET, BY THEIR DEFINITION, IS NOTHING BUT THE EXTERMINATION OF TIBETAN PEOPLE AND CULTURE.

SOON CHINA REVEALED TO ME ITS "TRUE COLORS".

I HAVE A PROPOSAL FOR YOU, SINCE YOU ARE THE BROTHER OF THE DALAI LAMA.

I WILL LET YOU GO BACK TO LHASA AS A FREE MAN, ON THE CONDITION THAT YOU CONVINCE THE DALAI LAMA TO ACCEPT CHINESE OCCUPATION.

IF HE DOES NOT ACCEPT IT... KILL HIM.

WHAT KIND OF PROPOSAL IS THAT? THAT'S RIDICULOUS!

AND OF COURSE, WE WILL COMPENSATE YOU GENEROUSLY.

KUNDUN, PLEASE LEAVE LHASA IMMEDIATELY! YOU SHOULD KNOW THAT I PRETENDED TO ACCEPT THEIR PROPOSAL SO I COULD VISIT YOU AND REVEAL THE TRUE INTENTIONS OF THE CHINESE ARMY OCCUPYING AMDO.

ARE YOU SUGGESTING THAT I SHOULD ESCAPE?

YOU ARE IN DANGER...

IF YOU ARE TAKEN HOSTAGE... WE WON'T BE ABLE TO RESIST CHINA WITH ARMED FORCE.

WHAT ARE YOU TALKING ABOUT? ARE YOU IMPLYING THAT TIBET SHOULD ENGAGE IN A WAR WITH CHINA?

AS I SEE IT, THERE IS NO OTHER WAY! I AM WILLING TO BREAK MY VOWS AS A MONK, TAKE MY ROBES OFF, AND RISK GOING ABROAD AS A SECRET MESSENGER TO GET SOME ARMED SUPPORT.

AMERICA IS THE FIRST NATION TO CONTACT. I BELIEVE THEY WOULD SUPPORT FREEING TIBET.

HOLD ON, BROTHER THUBTEN!!

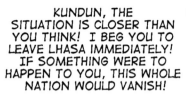

KUNDUN, THE SITUATION IS CLOSER THAN YOU THINK! I BEG YOU TO LEAVE LHASA IMMEDIATELY! IF SOMETHING WERE TO HAPPEN TO YOU, THIS WHOLE NATION WOULD VANISH!

BROTHER!!

.....

THE 13TH DALAI LAMA HAD TO SEEK POLITICAL ASYLUM TWICE IN HIS LIFE.

HE FIRST FLED THE COUNTRY WHEN THE BRITISH ARMY INVADED TIBET IN 1903, AND HAD TO FLEE A SECOND TIME WHEN THE QING DYNASTY TRIED TO OVERPOWER TIBET AGAIN IN 1910.

THE BRITISH ARMY DECIDED TO WITHDRAW SUDDENLY. AS FOR THE QING DYNASTY, THE TIBETAN ARMY SUCCESSFULLY FOUGHT AND REPELLED THEM IN THE WINTER OF 1911.

IMMEDIATELY AFTER THAT, THE PREVIOUS DALAI LAMA DECLARED TIBET'S INDEPENDENCE TO THE REST OF THE WORLD.

MAYBE IT IS TIME TO RE-EMXAMINE HIS WILL.

.....

UNLESS WE PROTECT
OUR OWN COUNTRY...

ALL THE RESPECTED
HOLDERS OF OUR FAITH
WILL DISAPPEAR AND
BECOME NAMELESS.

NOVEMBER 17, 1950.
ENTHRONEMENT
ON THIS DAY, I BECAME THE
OFFICIAL POLITICAL LEADER
OF TIBET.

MONKS AND THEIR
MONASTERIES WILL BE
DESTROYED.

THE LAWS WILL BE WEAKEND.

THE LAND AND PROPERTY
BELONGING TO GOVERNMENT
OFFICIALS WILL BE SEIZED.

THESE WORDS FROM
THE PREVIOUS DALAI
LAMA MEANT A LOT
TO ME, PARTICULARLY
AT THE AGE OF 15.

THEY THEMSELVES WILL BE FORCED TO SERVE THEIR ENEMIES OR WANDER THE COUNTRY LIKE BEGGARS.

KUNDUN, IT IS TIME FOR ME TO RETURN TO MY COUNTRY.

IT'S A PITY TO LET YOU GO, BUT AT THE SAME TIME, I WISH YOU A SAFE AND PLEASANT JOURNEY.

PLEASE ALWAYS KNOW THAT DURING THIS HARD TIME, THE REST OF THE WORLD IS WITH TIBET IN SPIRIT.

ALL BEINGS WILL BE SUNK IN GREAT HARDSHIP AND OVERWHELMING FEAR;

THE DAYS AND NIGHTS WILL DRAG ON SLOWLY IN SUFFERING.

"UNLESS WE PROTECT OUR OWN COUNTRY..." WHAT WILL HAPPEN...?

YOUR HOLINESS, PLEASE LEAVE LHASA FOR THE TIME BEING UNTIL WE HEAR FROM OUR MISSIONS, AND HAVE A SOLID PLAN OF ACTION.

PLEASE HURRY! THE CHINESE ARE REINFORCING THEIR ARMY IN THE EASTERN REGION AT THIS VERY MOMENT.

I WILL ENTRUST LEADERSHIP TO PRIME MINISTER *LOBSANG TASHI* AND PRIME MINISTER *LUKHANGWA* DURING MY ABSENCE. PLEASE TAKE CARE OF OUR NATION UNTIL I RETURN.

WE WILL NOT DISAPPOINT YOU, YOUR HOLINESS. WE WILL DO OUR ABSOLUTE BEST.

WHILE I SEEK TEMPORARY REFUGE IN **SOUTHERN TIBET**, LET'S HOPE THAT AMERICA, ENGLAND, INDIA, OR NEPAL WILL HEAR OUR PLEA AND WORK WITH US.

WE HAVE ALSO SENT A DELEGATION TO CONVINCE CHINA TO WITHDRAW.

OUR PATIENCE WILL BE TESTED, YOU KNOW.

YES, CERTAINLY!

WE UNDERSTAND!

YOU ARE TAKING HIS HOLINESS AWAY FROM US, AREN'T YOU?

KUNDUN, PLEASE DON'T LEAVE LHASA!

DON'T GIVE UP ON US! PLEASE COME BACK TO LHASA!

WE'RE JUST REGULAR TRAVELERS! THERE'S NO WAY HIS HOLINESS IS WITH US!

PLEASE, CALM DOWN!

LET US PASS THROUGH!

REST ASSURED. I HEARD THAT HIS ABSENCE WILL JUST BE TEMPORARY.

HE'S NOT DESERTING US COMPLETELY... I'M SURE HE'LL BE BACK SOON!

OTHER THAN THIS SAD ENCOUNTER, THE JOURNEY WENT SMOOTHLY.

A LOT OF PEOPLE TALKED TO ME CASUALLY, NEVER RECOGNIZING ME AS THE DALAI LAMA.

I TOOK THIS OPPORTUNITY TO COMMUNICATE WITH ORDINARY PEOPLE AS OFTEN AS POSSIBLE.

IN TALKING WITH THEM AND LEARNING HOW MUCH INJUSTICE THEY HAD BEEN ENDURING ON A DAILY BASIS, I CAME TO REALIZE THE URGENT NECESSITY OF POLITICAL REFORM.

IN JANUARY 1951, TWO WEEKS AFTER OUR DEPARTURE FROM LHASA, WE ARRIVED IN **DROMO** IN SOUTHERN TIBET.

HOW IS THAT POSSIBLE!? NONE OF OUR MISSIONS MADE IT TO THEIR DESTINATIONS?!

YES, CHINA WAS THE ONLY COUNTRY WE MANAGED TO REACH. AMERICA, ENGLAND, INDIA, AND NEPAL DID NOT ACCEPT OUR PLEA.

......

SO YOU'RE SAYING THAT TIBET HAS TO FACE CHINA'S MASSIVE STRENGTH ALL BY ITSELF...

I'VE BEEN THINKING ABOUT THE FACES OF THE MANY PEOPLE I MET DURING THE TRIP HERE.

THEIR LIVES ARE VERY SIMPLE, BUT HIGHLY SPIRITUAL, FILLED WITH APPRECIATION AND IN HARMONY WITH NATURE AND THE ENVIRONMENT EACH AND EVERY DAY.

DESPITE MATERIAL POVERTY, THEIR LIVES ARE RICH WITH RELIGIOUS FAITH, WITH THE BELIEF THAT THEY ARE CONNECTED TO THEIR ANCESTORS AS WELL AS TO THEIR FUTURE DESCENDANTS.

HOW CAN I PROTECT THESE PRECIOUS LIVES...? WILL I EVER BE CAPABLE OF DOING SO...?

YOUR HOLINESS, A REPORT FROM THE GOVERNOR OF THE KHAM PROVINCE, *NGAPOI NGAWANG JIGME*, JUST CAME IN.

WHAT DID NGAPOI SAY?

THE MAJORITY OF THE CHAMDO TERRITORY HAS FALLEN INTO THE HANDS OF THE CHINESE, AND BEFORE LONG THE LIBERATION ARMY WILL REACH LHASA. WE NEED TO START NEGOTIATING WITH CHINA VERY SOON, OTHERWISE...

NEGOTIATION!?

MORE THAN WE'VE ALREADY ATTEMPTED?

YES, THAT'S RIGHT. NGAPOI HAS SUGGESTED THAT HE VISIT BEIJING HIMSELF AND NEGOTIATE DIRECTLY WITH CHINA.

HE'S WILLING TO DO WHATEVER IT TAKES TO AVOID A WAR...

PLEASE CONTACT BOTH PRIME MINISTERS IN LHASA AND TELL THEM THIS INFORMATION...

YES, YOUR HOLINESS.

WE NEED TO DISPATCH OFFICERS FROM DROMO AND LHASA TO JOIN AND ASSIST NGAPOI IN CHINA IMMEDIATELY...

AND CLEARLY STATE THAT...

TIBET IS NOT ASKING FOR "EMANCIPATION," AS CHINA DEFINES IT. WE SIMPLY WANT TO MAINTAIN A PEACEFUL AND RESPECTFUL RELATIONSHIP WITH OUR GREAT NEIGHBOR.

BUT A FEW MONTHS LATER, IN MAY 1951, WE RECEIVED NEWS SO SHOCKING WE COULD NOT BELIEVE OUR EARS.

WE ARE HAPPY TO ANNOUNCE TODAY THAT REPRESENTATIVES OF THE CHINESE GOVERNMENT AND THE TIBETAN PROVINCE...

HAVE SIGNED A *SEVENTEEN-POINT "AGREEMENT"* FOR THE PEACEFUL LIBERATION OF TIBET.

HOW CAN THIS BE THE CASE!? I NEVER APPROVED SUCH AN AGREEMENT!!

CLAUSE ONE OF THE AGREEMENT STATES THAT "THE TIBETAN PEOPLE SHALL UNITE AND DRIVE OUT IMPERIALIST AGGRESSIVE FORCES FROM TIBET. THE TIBETAN PEOPLE WILL RETURN TO THE BIG FAMILY OF THE MOTHERLAND – THE PEOPLE'S REPUBLIC OF CHINA."

WHY...?

CLAUSE TWO STATES THAT "LOCAL GOVERNMENT OF TIBET WOULD ACTIVELY ASSIST THE PEOPLE'S LIBERATION ARMY TO ENTER TIBET AND CONSOLIDATE THE NATIONAL DEFENSE."

I DID NOT GIVE NGAPOI ANY AUTHORITY TO SIGN ANY DOCUMENTS, AND THE OFFICIAL SEALS OF STATE HAVE ALWAYS BEEN KEPT WITH ME.

THEY MUST HAVE FORGED THE SEAL, AND NGAPOI MUST HAVE BEEN COERCED.

THE NEGOTIATION WAS A CALCULATED PLOT FROM THE VERY BEGINNING!

WE JUST RECEIVED A TELEGRAM FROM GOVERNOR NGAPOI.

WHAT DID HE SAY?

HE SAID THAT THE NEW GOVERNOR-GENERAL OF TIBET, GENERAL *CHIANG CHIN-WU*, IS EN ROUTE TO HERE VIA INDIA.

GOVERNOR-GENERAL OF TIBET!?

THE TELEGRAM ONLY SUGGESTS THAT I MEET WITH GENERAL CHIANG. I ASSUME HE'S AFRAID TO WRITE ANYTHING MORE...

ARE THEY ANNOUNCING THAT THERE'S A NEW GOVERNOR OF TIBET!? WHO ON EARTH CREATED SUCH A POSITION?! NOBODY IN TIBET WOULD APPROVE THIS ACT!!

YOUR ELDEST BROTHER, TAKSTER RINPOCHE, ALSO WROTE TO YOU.

AGAIN HE IS SUGGESTING MY IMMEDIATE EVACUATION ABROAD.

KUNDUN, I HAVE GOOD NEWS! I HAVE ESTABLISHED CONTACT WITH THE AMERICAN CONSULATE IN CALCUTTA, AND HAVE MANAGED TO OBTAIN A VISA TO ENTER THE UNITED STATES.

THEY ARE SUPPORTIVE OF TIBET. THERE IS A GOOD CHANCE WE CAN WIN MILITARY AID FROM THE UNITED STATES!

IT IS TIME TO JOIN FORCES WITH AMERICANS AND FIGHT AGAINST CHINA!

SO THAT THIS CAN HAPPEN, PLEASE LEAVE TIBET AND MOVE TO INDIA IMMEDIATELY.

NO, BROTHER THUBTEN! THAT IS NOT POSSIBLE. I CANNOT LEAVE MY PEOPLE BEHIND!

RIGHT NOW, WE NEED TO WAIT FOR THE GENERAL'S ARRIVAL.

ALTHOUGH HE IS OUR ENEMY, HE IS A HUMAN BEING, JUST LIKE US... SO LET'S BELIEVE IN HIM AND WAIT AND SEE...

IT'S TRUE THAT HIS TROOPS HAVE KILLED MANY TIBETAN REBELS AND THEIR SUPPORTERS, BUT I DON'T THINK HE'S A BEAST WITH HORRIBLE HORNS ON HIS HEAD...

JULY 16, 1951
THE CHINESE DELEGATION ARRIVES IN DROMO

YOUR HOLINESS, PLEASE MEET GENERAL CHIANG CHIN-WU.

THE MEETING WILL PROCEED WITH THE HELP OF A CHINESE-TIBETAN INTERPRETER.

IT IS A GREAT HONOR TO MEET YOU, YOUR HOLINESS! FIRST OF ALL, ALLOW ME TO EXTEND THE VERY BEST REGARDS FROM CHAIRMAN MAO.

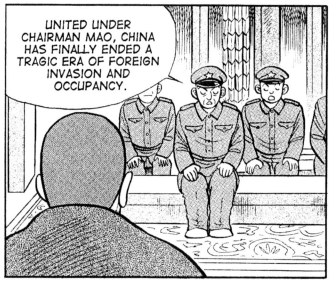 UNITED UNDER CHAIRMAN MAO, CHINA HAS FINALLY ENDED A TRAGIC ERA OF FOREIGN INVASION AND OCCUPANCY.

 YOU WILL NO LONGER SEE "OLD" CHINA, SUFFERING FROM POVERTY AND EXPLOITATION.

 COMMUNISM IS A SYSTEM, WHICH ENSURES GREATER *JUSTICE AND EQUALITY* AMONG ITS CITIZENS. CHINA WILL CONTINUE TO PROSPER, UNHAMPERED BY FOREIGN IMPERIALISTS.

 I REMEMBERED SEEING CHINESE PEOPLE STRUGGLING WHEN I WAS A LITTLE BOY.

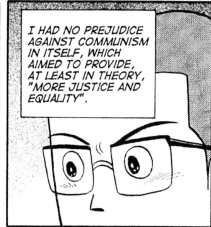 I HAD NO PREJUDICE AGAINST COMMUNISM IN ITSELF, WHICH AIMED TO PROVIDE, AT LEAST IN THEORY, "MORE JUSTICE AND EQUALITY".

BUT I WONDERED HOW IT WAS POSSIBLE FOR A COUNTRY THAT PURSUES SUCH A NOBLE THEORY TO ENGAGE IN SUCH DISRESPECTFUL ACTIONS TOWARDS OTHERS.

WE HAVE SIGNED THE SEVENTEEN-POINT AGREEMENT IN ORDER TO LIBERATE THE TIBETAN PEOPLE FROM THE HANDS OF THE IMPERIALISTS.

GENERAL CHIANG PROCEEDED TO EXPLAIN THE SITUATION AS IF THE AGREEMENT HAD BEEN MUTUALLY REACHED.

IN THE SEVENTEEN-POINT AGREEMENT, WE MADE IT CLEAR THAT TIBET HAS *AUTONOMY* TO GOVERN ITSELF, AND THAT CHINA RESPECTS THE AUTHORITY OF THE DALAI LAMA AND THE CURRENT POLITICAL STRUCTURE.

NEEDLESS TO SAY, WE WILL PRESERVE AND EMBRACE THE RELIGION, FAITH, AND CUSTOMS OF TIBET. MONASTERIES WILL ALSO BE PROTECTED.

AS WELL, WITH THIS AGREEMENT, WE SEEK TO IMPROVE EDUCATION AND AGRICULTURE, ENSURING THE WELFARE AND PROSPERITY OF THE TIBETAN PEOPLE.

THE AGREEMENT STATED THAT THE LIBERATION ARMY WOULD OCCUPY TIBET, AND THAT CHINA WOULD TAKE OVER TIBETAN DIPLOMACY.

PLEASE UNDERSTAND OUR GOOD INTENTIONS, AND RETURN PROMPTLY TO LHASA. WE LOOK FORWARD TO DISCUSSING THE AGREEMENT FURTHER!!

I KNEW THAT MY LIFE WOULD BE IN DANGER IN LHASA, BUT FELT THAT I NEEDED TO BE WITH OUR PEOPLE DURING THIS HARD TIME, AND MAKE SURE THAT THE CHINESE GENERAL WOULD KEEP HIS PROMISES.

ALTHOUGH IT'S HARD NOT TO HAVE DOUBTS OR APPREHENSION ABOUT THEIR INTENTIONS, LET'S STILL TRY TO HAVE FAITH IN WHAT THEY SAY.

YOU'RE GOING BACK TO LHASA!?

PLEASE DON'T! IT'S TOO DANGEROUS!

MY MISSION, FIRST AND FOREMOST, IS TO PROTECT MY PEOPLE.

WE MUST PREVENT MORE BLOODSHED.

LET'S KEEP OUR OPTIMISM UP AND HAVE HOPE IN DEALING WITH THE CHINESE.

END OF AUGUST, 1951
THE DALAI LAMA RETURNS FROM A TEMPORARY ASYLUM
IN SOUTHERN TIBET TO LHASA AFTER NINE MONTHS

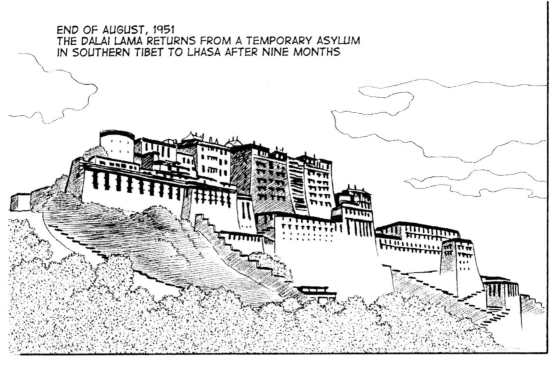

IT WAS THE
BEGINNING OF
EVEN MORE
SEVERE STRIFE...

A BATTALION OF MORE THAN
20,000 CHINESE SOLDIERS
HAD ARRIVED IN LHASA
(WHOSE ENTIRE POPULATION
IS 70,000).

ARE YOU OUT OF YOUR MIND!? YOU WANT US TO PREPARE AN ADDITIONAL 2000 TONS OF BARLEY FOR YOUR ARMY!?

THAT'S RIGHT! THE SEVENTEEN-POINT AGREEMENT CLEARLY STATES THAT FOOD SUPPLIES BE PROCURED LOCALLY. YOU MUST COOPERATE!

BUT...THAT'S... IMPOSSIBLE! SUCH A LARGE VOLUME OF BARLEY DOESN'T EVEN EXIST IN LHASA!

LHASA CITIZENS WILL EXPERIENCE NEAR-FAMINE IF THEY HAND OVER THEIR FOOD TO THE CHINESE TROOPS.

SINCE YOU PEOPLE ARRIVED, WE'RE FACING A SERIOUS FOOD SHORTAGE! GRAIN PRICES HAVE INCREASED TEN FOLD! PRICES OF OTHER COMMODITIES HAVE DOUBLED, OR IN SOME CASES, EVEN TRIPLED!

THE RELATIONSHIP BETWEEN THE CHINESE ARMY AND THE GENERAL PUBLIC WORSENED AS THE DAYS WENT ON.

THERE WERE WRITTEN PROTESTS AGAINST THE CHINESE MILITARY POSTED UP ALL OVER THE CITY.

WHAT KIND OF EMANCIPATION ARE THE CHINESE TALKING ABOUT? WHAT'S THE DIFFERENCE BETWEEN LIBERATING US AND INVADING US?

MANY MEETINGS WERE HELD ALL OVER THE PLACE, CRITICIZING THE CHINESE.

OUR NATION WAS A PEACEFUL COUNTRY WITH A BENEVOLENT GOVERNMENT BEFORE THE CHINESE INVADED US! WE WERE HAPPIER WITHOUT THEM!!

THAT'S RIGHT! THAT'S RIGHT! IS CHINA TRYING TO STARVE US?

WE DON'T NEED THIS SO-CALLED "LIBERATION"! CHINESE... GO HOME!!

SATIRICAL SONGS ABOUT THE CHINESE WERE HEARD ALL OVER THE CITY.

AND CHILDREN EVEN STARTED THROWING STONES AT THE CHINESE SOLDIERS.

CHINA IMMEDIATELY BANNED THESE ACTS OF PROTEST, WHILE THEY CONTINUED TO REPEATEDLY INFRINGE UPON THE AGREEMENT THEY HAD WRITTEN.

NOT ONLY WERE LAND AND BUILDINGS BELONGING TO CIVILIANS CONFISCATED, BUT THEY WERE USED TO ACCOMMODATE THE SOLDIERS. MANY FARMS WERE DESTROYED AND BECAME LAND FOR THE HIGHWAY LINK FROM TIBET TO BEIJING.

MANY TIBETANS WERE FORCED TO WORK ON THE CONSTRUCTION OF THE HIGHWAY, BEING PAID CLOSE TO NOTHING IN NEAR SLAVERY CONDITIONS.

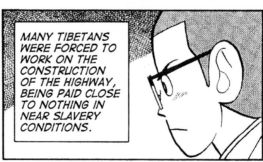

FURTHERMORE, MANY YOUTH FROM LHASA WERE SENT TO CHINA FOR EDUCATIONAL PROGRAMS THAT BRAINWASHED THEM TO HATE TIBETAN RELIGION, FAITH, CULTURE AND CUSTOMS.

ANGER ABOUT CHINESE COLONIAL POLICIES INTENSIFIED EACH DAY AMONG THE CITIZENS OF LHASA.

AND THEN FINALLY...

WHAT ON EARTH IS THIS?!

PRIME MINSTER LUKHANGWA! PRIME MINSTER LOBSANG TASHI! YOU MUST BE THE MASTER MINDS BEHIND THIS!!

HOW CAN I BE OF ASSISTANCE TO YOU?

A GROUP WHO CALLED THEMSELVES "THE REPRESENTATIVES OF THE CITIZENS" JUST SENT US THIS NOTE DETAILING THE SO-CALLED "*SIX-POINT MEMORANDUM*".

IT IS AN OUTRAGEOUS NOTE CRITICIZING US AND DEMANDING THE WITHDRAWAL OF OUR TROOPS!

THIS MUST BE A PART OF YOUR CONSPIRATORIAL PLOT!!

YOU CUNNING IMPERIALISTS!

THE NOTE HAS NOTHING TO DO WITH US!

DON'T CALL US "IMPERIALISTS!!"

IF YOU CLAIM THAT YOU AREN'T...

THEN YOU SHOULDN'T HAVE ANY PROBLEMS COOPERATING WITH US...

... AND MERGING THE TIBETAN ARMY WITH THE LIBERATION ARMY!

WHAT!?

YOU MUST BE OUT OF YOUR MIND!

IT IS SIMPLY OUT OF THE QUESTION FOR THE TIBETAN ARMY TO GIVE THEIR LOYALTY TO THE LIBERATION ARMY WHICH, MAY I REMIND YOU, INVADED TIBET!

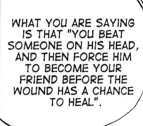

WHAT YOU ARE SAYING IS THAT "YOU BEAT SOMEONE ON HIS HEAD, AND THEN FORCE HIM TO BECOME YOUR FRIEND BEFORE THE WOUND HAS A CHANCE TO HEAL".

YOU'RE THE ONES WHO ARE OUT OF YOUR MINDS! THIS IS A PART OF THE SEVENTEEN-POINT AGREEMENT! YOU'RE BREACHING THE AGREEMENT!

LOOK WHO'S TALKING! THE AGREEMENT CLEARLY STATES THAT THE TIBETAN REGIONAL GOVERNMENT CAN CARRY OUT ITS REFORMS BY ITS OWN INITIATIVE, AND THAT THE CHINESE AUTHORITIES CANNOT FORCE THEM TO DO OTHERWISE.

SHUT UP! I'M CONVINCED THAT YOU'RE IMPERIALISTIC ANTI-REVOLUTIONALISTS, AFTER ALL!

I DEMAND THAT THE DALAI LAMA REMOVE YOU TWO FROM THE CABINET.

DON'T THINK THAT YOU CAN GET AWAY WITH THIS!!

EARLY SPRING, 1953

BEFORE LONG, AN OFFICIAL DOCUMENT DEMANDING THE REMOVAL OF THE TWO PRIME MINISTERS ARRIVED. THE NEXT MORNING, BOTH OF THEM ASKED ME TO ACCEPT THEIR RESIGNATION.

I UNDERSTAND... DO OTHER CABINET MEMBERS HAVE ANY OBJECTIONS REGARDING THEIR RESIGNATIONS?

I AM VERY SORRY TO LET GO OF SUCH HARDWORKING AND FAITHFUL PRIME MINISTERS...

HOWEVER, I ALSO UNDERSTAND THAT KEEPING YOU IN YOUR CURRENT POSITIONS WOULD IN FACT JEOPARDIZE YOUR LIVES.

IT CANNOT BE HELPED... I HEREBY ACCEPT YOUR RESIGNATIONS.

HOWEVER, WE CANNOT JUST LIE DOWN AND SURRENDER TO CHINA.

WE SHOULD PRESENT OUR OWN CONCRETE REFORM PLANS TO THE CHINESE, INSTEAD OF FOLLOWING THEIR INFLUENCE.

LET'S ASSEMBLE OUR OWN REFORM COMMITTEE AT ONCE!

ESTABLISHMENT OF A DEMOCRATIC JUDICIARY SYSTEM... IMPROVEMENT OF THE EDUCATION SYSTEM... MAJOR LAND REFORMS... WE HAVE SO MUCH AHEAD OF US TO DO!

IT IS TIME TO UTILIZE THE GUARANTEE OF TIBETAN AUTONOMY AS CLEARLY STATED ON THE SEVENTEEN-POINT AGREEMENT.

NEVERTHELESS, ALL OF OUR REFORM PLANS WERE REJECTED BY THE CHINESE.

YOUR HOLINESS, THE *PANCHEN LAMA* HAS ARRIVED.

APRIL 28, 1952,
THE PANCHEN LAMA
ARRIVES IN LHASA

YOUR HOLINESS,
IT IS MY HONOR
TO FINALLY
MEET YOU.

THE 10TH
PANCHEN LAMA
15 YEARS OLD

I HAVE BEEN
LOOKING FORWARD
TO THIS DAY.

THE PANCHEN LAMA IS
THE HIGHEST SPIRITUAL
LEADER OF TIBET NEXT
TO THE DALAI LAMA.

THE PLEASURE
IS MINE,
YOUR HOLINESS.

I OFTEN COME HERE AND WATCH OUR PEOPLE LIVING THEIR LIVES.

YOU WISH FOR THEIR HAPPINESS, DON'T YOU?

ABSOLUTELY. THAT'S OUR MISSION.

I ALWAYS KEEP THAT IN MIND WHEN I PRACTICE MY RELIGIOUS AUSTERITIES.

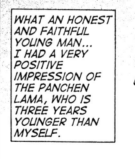

WHAT AN HONEST AND FAITHFUL YOUNG MAN... I HAD A VERY POSITIVE IMPRESSION OF THE PANCHEN LAMA, WHO IS THREE YEARS YOUNGER THAN MYSELF.

HE HAD A CERTAIN AIR OF INNOCENCE ABOUT HIM, AND SEEMED A VERY HAPPY AND PLEASANT PERSON.

AT THE SAME TIME, I NOTICED THAT HE WAS ALWAYS ACCOMPANIED BY UNIFORMED SECURITY OFFICERS.

UNFORTUNATELY, HE HAD BEEN BROUGHT UP SINCE INFANCY UNDER THE STRICT SURVEILLANCE OF THE CHINESE GOVERNMENT.

ARE YOU HEADING TO SHIGATSE NOW?

YES. I PLAN TO SPEND SOME TIME AT THE TASHILHUNPHO MONASTERY.

I'M REALLY LOOKING FORWARD TO THE VISIT.

AT THAT MOMENT, NEITHER ONE OF US, WITH OUR SIMILARLY ODD CHILDHOODS, COULD EVER HAVE GUESSED HOW STRIKINGLY DIFFERENTLY OUR LIVES WOULD UNFOLD.

5. LEFT
6. ABOVE
Taking refuge in Southern Tibet,
nearby the border of India in 1950

7. BELOW
Meeting with the Indian Prime Minster,
Nehru with the Panchen Lama in 1956

Source: Tibet Religious Foundation of His Holiness the Dalai Lama

| 8. ABOVE | 9. BELOW | Source: |
| A visit to Beijing in 1954 | Meeting with Mao Zedong in Beijing | Tibet Religious Foundation of His Holiness the Dalai Lama |

SEPTEMBER, 1954
BEIJING, CHINA

FLASH

FLASH

FLASH

THE PANCHEN LAMA AND I WERE INVITED BY THE COMMUNIST PARTY TO ATTEND THE **NATIONAL PEOPLE'S CONGRESS** BEING HELD IN BEIJING.

THE TIBETAN PEOPLE WERE STRONGLY OPPOSED TO THE IDEA THAT I VISIT BEIJING.

FLASH

FLASH

SOON AFTER OUR ARRIVAL IN BEIJING, CHAIRMAN MAO AND I HAD A PRIVATE MEETING WITH THE HELP OF AN INTERPRETER.

YOU HAVE A MARVELOUS HISTORY. MANY, MANY MOONS AGO, YOU EVEN CONQUERED MUCH OF CHINA.

BUT NOW YOU HAVE FALLEN BEHIND, AND WE WANT TO HELP YOU.

IN TWENTY YEARS' TIME YOU COULD BE AHEAD OF US, AND THEN IT WILL BE YOUR TURN TO HELP CHINA.

THE FIRST STEP TO REFORM IS FOR YOU TO ASSEMBLE A PREPARATORY COMMITTEE. THE PEOPLE IN THE COMMITTEE SHOULD REPRESENT THE WILL OF THE TIBETAN PEOPLE.

THE REFORMS SHOULD BE CARRIED OUT AT A SPEED THAT TIBETAN PEOPLE FEEL COMFORTABLE WITH.

IF OUR PEOPLE IGNORE YOUR OPINIONS AND ARE HASTY WITH THE REFORMS, PLEASE LET ME KNOW.

I WILL RECALL THEM TO CHINA AND PUNISH THEM ACCORDINGLY.

I FELT A SMALL GLIMMER OF HOPE. I STARTED TO TAKE SERIOUSLY A POSSIBLE ALLIANCE WITH COMMUNIST CHINA.

I WOULD LIKE TO LEARN CHINESE LANGUAGE WHILE I AM HERE. DO YOU HAVE ANY TUTORS THAT YOU CAN RECOMMEND?

YES, WE DO, YOUR HOLINESS. LET US ARRANGE ONE FOR YOU.

HOWEVER, STRANGELY...

AT THE NATIONAL PEOPLE'S CONGRESS, PARTICIPANTS DID NOT SEEM TO BE EXPRESSING WHAT WAS REALLY ON THEIR MINDS.

TO MY EYES, THE NON-COMMUNISTS SEEMED TO BE DOING NOTHING BUT FLATTERING COMMUNIST PARTY MEMBERS.

THOUGH I HAD BEEN APPOINTED VICE-CHAIRMAN OF THE STANDING COMMITTEE OF THE NATIONAL PEOPLE'S CONGRESS, I HAD VIRTUALLY NO AUTHORITY, AND WONDERED WHY I HAD BEEN INVITED TO THIS GATHERING IN THE FIRST PLACE...

I ALSO WONDERED ABOUT THE RESTRICTIONS ON WHERE I COULD GO AND WHOM I COULD MEET. THE CHINESE NEVER ALLOWED ME TO INTERACT WITH ANY "ORDINARY" CHINESE CITIZENS.

THE ONLY TIME I WAS ALLOWED TO GO OUTSIDE WAS TO VISIT THE RAPIDLY DEVELOPING INDUSTRIAL AREAS.

ALL THESE MYSTERIES MADE SENSE ALL OF A SUDDEN...

YOUR HOLINESS!

WE SAW THE PICTURE OF YOU LEAVING LHASA FOR BEIJING IN THE NEWSPAPER!

I WAS SURPRISED TO SEE THAT THE TIBETAN PEOPLE SAW YOU OFF TO CHINA WITH SUCH DELIGHT AND ENTHUSIASM. I WAS GLAD TO SEE THAT.

WHAT!?

THAT'S COMPLETELY UNTRUE! THE TIBETANS OBJECTED TO MY VISITING CHINA!

IT CAN'T BE TRUE!

SO MANY PEOPLE WERE TERRIFIED, AND WERE GRIEVING ABOUT MY NEVER RETURNING HOME...

YOU ARE SAYING THAT THE REPORTS ABOUT YOUR VISIT ARE FULL OF LIES?

I FINALLY SEE THAT MY VISIT TO CHINA WAS MEANT TO CHANGE THEIR NEGATIVE IMAGE IN THE EYES OF THE REST OF THE WORLD, AND AT THE SAME TIME DEMONSTRATE THAT THEY ARE NOT AGGRESSORS.

HAVING REALIZED THEIR HIDDEN AGENDA, I DECIDED TO GO BACK HOME. IT HAD BEEN A LONG TIME SINCE I HAD LEFT LHASA IN THE SUMMER.

THEY DON'T MIND LYING FOR THEIR OWN PURPOSES, DO THEY?

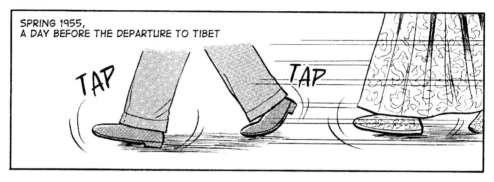

SPRING 1955,
A DAY BEFORE THE DEPARTURE TO TIBET

TAP

TAP

HERE HE
IS, SIR!

GREAT TO SEE
YOU AGAIN,
YOUR HOLINESS.

I HEARD THAT YOU
ARE GOING BACK TO
LHASA TOMORROW,
SO I ASSUME THAT
THIS WILL BE OUR
LAST MEETING.
I HAVE SOME
ADVICE FOR YOU.

I'M SORRY
THAT WE COULD
NOT ARRANGE
AN INTERPRETER
IN TIME...

NO PROBLEM.
ACTUALLY, I
HAVE BEEN
LEARNING
CHINESE...

IT IS IMPORTANT FOR THE FUTURE
OF TIBET THAT THEY CONVENE AN
OFFICIAL CONGRESSIONAL BODY
AS SOON AS POSSIBLE, AND THEN
LET THE REPRESENTATIVES RECEIVE
THE PEOPLE'S OPINIONS.

I AM CONFIDENT THAT YOU HAVE LEARNED A GREAT DEAL IN BEIJING.

YES, THANK YOU.

YOUR OPEN-MINDED ATTITUDE IS TRULY INSPIRATIONAL...

HAVING SAID THIS, I WOULD LIKE YOU TO KNOW ONE THING BEFORE YOU GO...

YOU KNOW...

RELIGION IS POISON.

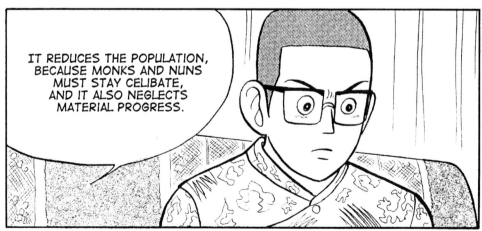

IT REDUCES THE POPULATION, BECAUSE MONKS AND NUNS MUST STAY CELIBATE, AND IT ALSO NEGLECTS MATERIAL PROGRESS.

APRIL 1956,
INSIDE THE NEW MUNICIPAL HALL
IN FRONT OF THE POTALA PALACE

IT IS MY GREAT PLEASURE TO CELEBRATE THE INAUGURATION OF THE **PREPARATORY COMMITTEE FOR THE AUTONOMOUS REGION OF TIBET (PCART)** AT THIS NEW MUNICIPAL HALL THAT WE, THE CHINESE, BUILT.

AS SOON AS I ARRIVED IN LHASA FROM CHINA, I ASSEMBLED PCART, AS CHAIRMAN MAO HAD SUGGESTED.

THE ONLY WAY TO BRING THE TIBETAN STANDARD OF LIVING UP TO THAT OF THE CHINESE IS TO FOLLOW THE REFORM PLANS THAT PCART PROPOSES!

THE DAY WAS VERY FESTIVE.
A CHINESE MILITARY BAND
PLAYED AND COMMUNIST
SONGS WERE SUNG.
THE MUNICIPAL HALL WAS
DECORATED WITH FLAGS AND
BANNERS DISPLAYING
CHAIRMAN MAO AND
HIS COLLEAGUES.

IRONICALLY, THAT SCENE ENCAPSULATED WHAT PCART REALLY REPRESENTED.

SINCE PCART HAD BEEN PUT IN PLACE, THE POLITICAL SITUATION IN EASTERN TIBET HAD WORSENED.

IN KHAM PROVINCE, EASTERN TIBET

LOOK CLOSELY! CHAIRMAN MAO, THE DALAI LAMA, AND THE PANCHEN LAMA ARE STANDING SIDE-BY-SIDE, WITH SMILES ON THEIR FACES.

HOW COULD YOU POSSIBLY DISOBEY THE INSTRUCTIONS OF PCART?

PCART HAS DECIDED THAT TIBETAN FARMERS SHOULD CHANGE THEIR FARMING METHODS TO THOSE OF THE CHINESE.

BOTH THE DALAI LAMA AND THE PANCHEN LAMA APPROVED THESE REFORM PLANS.

YOU CAN'T BE OPPOSED TO THE REFORMS! IF YOU ARE, THEN YOU ARE ANTI-REVOLUTIONARY CRIMINALS! WE HAVE NO MERCY FOR SUCH PEOPLE.

PADAP   PADAP

YOUR HOLINESS, I MUST SHOW YOU SOMETHING!

WHAT'S GOING ON? YOU'RE SO UPSET!

THIS IS A NEWSPAPER THAT THE CHINESE OFFICIALS PUBLISHED IN KHAM. THE CAPTION CALLED THESE PEOPLE "REACTIONARY CRIMINALS".

HOW COULD THEY DO SUCH A THING?!

EVER SINCE PCART BEGAN, THE CHINESE AUTHORITIES HAD STARTED THREATENING AND SUPPRESSING PEOPLE WHO DID NOT LISTEN TO THEM IN KHAM.

IN CHAMDO, A GROUP OF DISSENTERS WERE CONFINED IN THE JOMDHA DZONG FORT FOR TWO WEEKS.

SOME OF THEM MANAGED TO ESCAPE FROM THE CHINESE TROOPS SURROUNDING THE FORT. LATER, THEY BECAME LEADERS OF *THE FREEDOM FIGHTERS' ALLIANCE MOVEMENT*, AND AS SUCH HAVE TROUBLED THE CHINESE AUTHORITIES.

SUMMER 1956. CHINA LAUNCHED A MAJOR COUNTERATTACK AGAINST THE FREEDOM FIGHTERS BY BOMBING THE RETING MONASTERY IN KHAM.

BLAAAM

THE ATTACK BY THE CHINESE ARMY ESCALATED TO THE AERIAL BOMBING OF THE TOWN AND LOCAL TEMPLES.

BRAAAM

BRAAAM

AS A RESULT, THOUSANDS OF TEMPLES AND TOWNS WERE COMPLETELY DESTROYED.

DECLARE IT
IN FRONT OF
THE PUBLIC!

"SWEAR THAT YOU WILL
RELINQUISH YOUR CELIBACY!
TELL THEM THAT YOU WILL
COMMIT A MURDER!"

NO LOGIC WILL EVER JUSTIFY THE SLAUGHTER OF WOMEN, CHILDREN AND MONKS...NOT TO MENTION THE BOMBINGS OF OUR MONASTERIES.

WELL...

I'M GOING TO WRITE TO CHAIRMAN MAO. HE WILL TAKE STRONG MEASURES AGAINST THE SUBORDINATES WHO DO NOT LISTEN TO HIS INSTRUCTIONS!

MONTHS LATER...

HAVE WE HEARD FROM CHAIRMAN MAO?

CHAIRMAN MAO DOES NOT EVEN REPLY TO ME...

WHY... IT HAS BEEN A WHILE, HASN'T IT....

WHAT YOU ARE DOING IS ATROCIOUS!

THE SEVENTEEN-POINT AGREEMENT IS MEANINGLESS! PCART HAS BECOME A VEHICLE FOR LOOTING AND SLAUGHTERING.

AT THE END OF NOVEMBER 1956, I WAS INVITED BY A RELIGIOUS SOCIETY TO ATTEND THE **BUDDHA JAYANTI** CELEBRATION, MARKING THE 2,500TH BIRTH ANNIVERSARY OF LORD BUDDHA. I WENT TO INDIA WHERE THE CEREMONY WAS HELD.

NORTH EAST INDIA

CONSIDERING THE STRICT SURVEILLANCE I ENDURED UNDER CHINESE OCCUPATION, IT WAS ALMOST A MIRACLE THAT I WAS ABLE TO TRAVEL ABROAD.

THE TEACHINGS OF THE LORD BUDDHA COULD LEAD NOT ONLY TO PEACE IN THE LIVES OF INDIVIDUALS,

BUT ALSO TO PEACE BETWEEN NATIONS.

AFTER SPEAKING AT BUDDHA JAYANTI, I VISITED **BODH GAYA,** WHERE BUDDHA ATTAINED ENLIGHTENMENT.

I WAS ABLE TO GIVE MYSELF WHOLLY TO DEEP FEELINGS OF JOY AND VENERATION THERE.

KUNDUN, PLEASE DO NOT RETURN TO LHASA. PLEASE STAY IN INDIA...

WE STRONGLY ADVISE THAT YOU STAY INDIA AND SEEK FURTHER SUPPORT FROM FOREIGN GOVERNMENTS.

BUT THE SITUATION IN TIBET WENT FROM BAD TO WORSE IN THE MEANTIME. THOSE AROUND ME WERE DEBATING WHETHER OR NOT I SHOULD REMAIN IN INDIA.

TWO OF MY BROTHERS, WHOM I HAD NOT SEEN FOR A LONG TIME, JOINED THE DISCUSSION IN CALCUTTA.

IF IT HAD NOT BEEN FOR THE BUDDHA JAYANTI, I WOULD NOT HAVE BEEN ABLE TO COME TO INDIA OR LEAVE LHASA.

AS EXPECTED, MANY TRIED TO CONVINCE ME TO STAY.

BROTHER THUBTEN... WHAT DO YOU MEAN BY "SUPPORT FROM A FOREIGN GOVERNMENT"? ARE YOU REFERRING TO AMERICA?

YES, KUNDUN! AMERICA WILL SUPPORT US!

BUT IF WE GET SOME SUPPORT FROM AMERICA, THERE WILL BE ARMED CONFLICT FOR SURE!

DOES KUNDUN KNOW THAT WE ARE CONTACTING THE *CIA*?

NO, NOBODY HAS TOLD HIM YET...

THE OTHER DAY, I MADE A PILGRIMAGE TO RAJ GHAT ON THE BANKS OF THE JAMUNA RIVER, WHERE *MAHATMA GANDHI* WAS CREMATED.

WITH HIS PEOPLE, LIKE OURS, ENDURING FOREIGN OCCUPATION, HE ADVOCATED THE DOCTRINE OF *NON-VIOLENCE*, AND EVENTUALLY WON INDEPENDENCE FOR INDIA.

I AM CONVINCED THAT HIS DEVOTION TO THE CAUSE OF NON-VIOLENCE IS THE ONLY WAY TO CONDUCT POLITICS.

WE WILL NEVER DEFEAT CHINA TODAY WITH "NON-VIOLENCE!!"

KUNDUN, GOING INTO BATTLE IS THE ONLY WAY WE CAN WIN BACK OUR INDEPENDENCE!

WAR ONLY CREATES ENDLESS HATRED. EVEN IF YOU WIN A BATTLE, HOW CAN YOU POSSIBLY BUILD A HEALTHY NATION, HAVING CREATED SO MUCH HATRED IN THE PROCESS...? HOW CAN WE SUSTAIN A NEW RELATIONSHIP WITH CHINA?

THE HATRED WILL NEVER COMPLETELY FADE AWAY...

SUMMER 1957, THE DALAI LAMA RETURNS TO LHASA

THROUGHOUT THE KHAM AND AMDO REGIONS, TIBETAN FREEDOM FIGHTERS AND THE CHINESE ARMY ARE ENGAGING IN FULL-FLEDGED WARFARE!

TOWNS AND VILLAGES NOW LIE IN RUINS FROM BOMBINGS AND BOMBARDMENTS.

THE WAR WILL SOON SPREAD, AFFECTING THE WHOLE OF CENTRAL TIBET.

THE FREEDOM FIGHTERS NUMBER SEVERAL TENS OF THOUSANDS, AND THEY ARE HANGING IN THERE. MOST OF THEIR WEAPONS SEEM TO BE SUPPLIED BY THE UNITED STATES CIA.

THE CIA!? YOU MEAN AMERICANS ARE GIVING MONEY AND WEAPONS TO THE GUERRILLAS?

I HAVE HEARD THAT THE AMERICANS ARE DROPPING SECONDHAND WEAPONS USED BY THE ENGLISH ARMY INSTEAD OF THEIR OWN, SO THAT THEY CAN REMAIN ANONYMOUS.

THEIR MOTIVE IS NOT TO SUPPORT THE INDEPENDENCE OF TIBET, BUT TO PREVENT THE SPREAD OF COMMUNISM.

ONCE THEY FULFILL THEIR INTERESTS, THEY WILL IMMEDIATELY BACK AWAY FROM THE CONFLICT.

YOUR HOLINESS!

PLEASE CALL UP THE TIBETAN ARMY RIGHT AWAY, AND HELP US SUPPRESS THE REBELLION!

THAT IS NOT POSSIBLE.

WHY NOT!? THE REBELS ARE ALREADY TWO DAYS AWAY FROM LHASA!!

IF WE DISPATCH THE TIBETAN ARMY TODAY, I AM SURE THAT THEY WILL TAKE SIDES WITH THE FREEDOM FIGHTERS.

HOW UNGRATEFUL! DO TIBETANS ALWAYS RESPOND TO SUCH KINDNESS WITH A LACK OF GRATITUDE?!

WHAT KIND OF KINDNESS ARE YOU TALKING ABOUT?

AS I FELT THIS CATASTROPHE FAST APPROACHING, I MOVED THE DATE OF MY FINAL EXAMINATION FOR MY DOCTORATE OF BUDDHIST STUDIES FORWARD, TO THE SAME DAY AS THE MONLAM GREAT PRAYER FESTIVAL, A YEAR AND A HALF AWAY.

I HAVE TO PASS THE EXAM TO BE OFFICIALLY APPROVED AS A MONK AS SOON AS POSSIBLE...

... AND BECOME A TRUE SPIRITUAL LEADER OF TIBET.

DALAI LAMA 23 YEARS OLD

PLEASE BLESS ME ON BEHALF OF OUR PEOPLE...

ONE YEAR LATER NEW YEAR, 1959

YOUR HOLINESS, ARE YOU INTERESTED IN A DANCE PERFORMANCE?

YES, I AM.

THAT'S GOOD NEWS! WE WILL BE RECEIVING A NEW CHINESE DANCE TROUPE IN LHASA SHORTLY.

WE HAVE MADE A SPECIAL SEATING ARRANGEMENT FOR YOU TO SEE THE PERFORMANCE WITH A BETTER VIEW.

THANK YOU FOR THE INVITATION. I WILL ATTEND THE SHOW ON MARCH 10TH, AFTER THE MONLAM FESTIVAL.

I LOOK FORWARD TO SEEING YOU THERE THEN!

A FEW DAYS BEFORE MARCH 10, I RECEIVED MY DOCTORAL DEGREE AND THE TITLE OF **GESHE**, UNANIMOUSLY APPROVED BY THE PANEL OF JUDGES.

THOUSANDS OF SPECTATORS GATHERED AND CELEBRATED MY ACHIEVEMENT ALONG THE ROAD FROM THE **JOKHANG TEMPLE** (WHERE THE EXAMINATION WAS HELD) ALL THE WAY TO MY PALACE.

MARCH 7

THAT MOMENT OF GRATITUDE LASTED ONLY BRIEFLY...

YOUR HOLINESS, PLEASE DECLINE THE INVITATION TO GO TO TOMORROW'S PERFORMANCE!

EARLIER TODAY, OUR COMMANDING OFFICER WAS TOLD BY THE CHINESE AUTHORITIES THAT ONLY A FEW BODYGUARDS COULD ACCOMPANY YOUR HOLINESS TO THE SHOW!

EVERYTHING SHOULD BE CARRIED OUT IN STRICT SECRECY!

YOUR YOUNGER BROTHER WAS ALSO INVITED, AND WAS TOLD TO COME FROM THE DREPUNG MONASTERY UNACCOMPANIED.

ALSO, THEY HAVE ANNOUNCED THAT THERE WILL BE TRAFFIC RESTRICTIONS AROUND THE STONE BRIDGE THAT LEADS OVER THE RIVER NEAR THE CHINESE HEADQUARTERS.

SOMETHING IS DEFINITELY NOT RIGHT HERE!!!

YOUR HOLINESS! THIS IS SURELY SOME SORT OF PLOT! IF YOU AND YOUR YOUNGER BROTHER GO TO THE PERFORMANCE, I AM AFRAID THAT YOU ARE PUTTING YOUR LIVES AT RISK! PLEASE DON'T GO!

NO, I CAN'T DO THAT. IF I REJECT THEIR INVITATION, IT MIGHT HAVE NEGATIVE CONSEQUENCES. THEY MAY EVEN CLAIM A BREACH OF DIPLOMACY!

I WILL BRING A HANDFUL OF STAFF, AND HOPEFULLY THINGS WILL GO SMOOTHLY.

MOST IMPORTANTLY, WE MUST NOT LET THIS NEWS LEAK OUT TO THE PUBLIC.

OTHERWISE, THERE WILL BE CHAOS.

HOWEVER...

CHEEP CHEEEP

IN THE END, IT WAS IMPOSSIBLE TO KEEP THIS ARRANGEMENT A SECRET...

MARCH 11, 1959, EARLY MORNING NORBULINGKA PALACE

WHAT'S GOING ON?!

THE CROWD IS GETTING BIGGER AND BIGGER!! IT WILL SOON TURN INTO A RIOT!

.....

WE WERE UNABLE TO WITHHOLD YOUR PLAN TO ATTEND THE PERFORMANCE TODAY.

YOUR HOLINESS! PLEASE DON'T GO TO THE PERFORMANCE AT THE CHINESE HEADQUARTERS TODAY!!

TRAITOR! HOW COULD YOU RIDE IN A CAR BELONGING TO THE CHINESE ARMY!!

SHAME ON YOU!

GIVE TIBET BACK TO THE TIBETAN PEOPLE!!

CHINESE, GO HOME!!

!

THE CROWD AROUND THE PALACE IS GROWING TO 30,000, AND THEY ARE BARRICADING THE ENTRANCE TO THE IMPERIAL VILLA. NO CABINET MEMBERS OR GOVERNMENT OFFICIALS ARE ABLE TO GET INTO THE BUILDING!

EVERYBODY OUTSIDE IS TRYING TO PROTECT YOUR HOLINESS FROM THE CHINESE ARMY!

THE CROWD MAY ATTACK THE STATIONARY TROOPS AT ANY MOMENT!

WE MUST PREVENT THAT FROM HAPPENING!!

IF THAT HAPPENS, THE CHINESE ARMY WILL TAKE ADVANTAGE OF THE SITUATION AND STRIKE BACK EVEN HARDER, AND TENS OF THOUSANDS OF PEOPLE WOULD LOSE THEIR LIVES.

LHASA WILL BECOME A LAND OF DESTRUCTION, JUST AS THE CHINESE WISH.

IN OTHER WORDS...

THE NATION KNOWN AS TIBET WOULD VANISH...

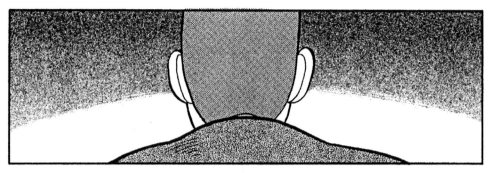

I WILL CANCEL MY PLAN AND PULL OUT FROM ATTENDING THE PERFORMANCE TODAY.

PLEASE IMMEDIATELY ASK THE CHINESE OFFICIALS TO EXCUSE US FROM ATTENDING. IN THE MEAN TIME, I WILL TRY TO PACIFY THE CROWD SURROUNDING THE PALACE.

HOW DARE YOU CHANGE YOUR MIND AT THE LAST MOMENT, YOU IMPERIALIST REBEL! I KNOW THE TIBETAN GOVERNMENT IS SECRETLY CREATING AN UPHEAVAL BY PROVOKING THE CROWD!!

PLEASE BE QUIET, EVERYONE! REST ASSURED THAT HIS HOLINESS IS NOT GOING TO THE PERFORMANCE!

HE WISHES FOR YOU ALL TO MAKE YOUR WAY HOME, QUIETLY!

IT'S IMPOSSIBLE! THE CROWD ISN'T LEAVING!

PLEASE UNDERSTAND... YOUR PROTESTING INVITES AN EVEN GREATER DANGER...

THE CHINESE ARMY IS REARRANGING ITS FORMATION! WE MAY HAVE A VIOLENT CONFRONTATION AT ANY MOMENT!!

WOULD YOU FIND THE LEADERS OF THE CROWD AND BRING THEM HERE?

MARCH 13

YOU MUST KNOW THIS! THE CHINESE ARMY IS ABOUT TO RESORT TO ARMED FORCE TO DEAL WITH THE SITUATION!

PLEASE BREAK UP THE CROWD IMMEDIATELY!

IT IS YOUR DUTY AS LEADERS TO AVOID THE WORST POSSIBLE SCENARIO!!

MARCH.16

TIBET NO LONGER APPROVES CHINESE AUTHORITY!

LET'S PROTECT THE DALAI LAMA FROM THE CHINESE ARMY!

YOUR HOLINESS, NGAPOI JUST SECRETLY SENT YOU THIS REPORT FROM CHINESE MILITARY HEADQUARTERS.

WHAT IS IT, YOUR HOLINESS!?

NGAPOI SAYS THAT THE CHINESE ARE GOING TO ATTACK THE CROWD AND SHELL NORBULINGKA!

HE ALSO SUGGESTED THAT I INDICATE WHERE I WILL BE ON THE MAP, SO HE COULD MAKE THE ARTILLERY MEN AVOID SHELLING NEAR ME...

I CAN'T BELIEVE THIS! NOT ONLY MY OWN LIFE, BUT ALSO TENS OF THOUSANDS OF LIVES ARE ABOUT TO BE TAKEN AWAY, AS WELL...

HOW CAN WE DISSOLVE THE CROWD AND SEND THEM HOME SAFELY...? IS THERE ANY WAY, I WONDER...?

IT WILL BE EXTREMELY DIFFICULT! THEIR ANGER AGAINST THE DICTATORIAL FOREIGN CONQUEROR HAS REACHED ITS LIMIT.

THEY WILL REMAIN THERE NO MATTER HOW LONG IT TAKES, AND ARE WILLING TO DIE FOR THE SAKE OF GUARDING THEIR *"PRECIOUS PROTECTOR"*.

HOW CAN I RESCUE THEM?... HOW CAN THEY BE CONVINCED TO DISPERSE AND LEAVE THE NORBULINGKA PALACE...?

IT'S TO DO WITH ME. I SHOULD NOT BE HERE...

IF I'M NOT HERE, THEY WON'T HAVE A REASON TO STAY AND PROTEST!

THAT'S RIGHT! THE ONLY WAY TO RESOLVE THIS SITUATION IS FOR ME TO EVACUATE!!

LEAVE!
LEAVE HERE
TONIGHT!!

HEY, CHECK THIS OUT! THIS IS A ROUTE FROM NORBULINGKA DOWN TO THE LAST TIBETAN TOWN ON THE INDIAN BORDER!

THERE SEEMS TO BE NO ALTERNATIVE...

MARCH 17

MOTHER, *TENDZIN*. PLEASE LEAVE BEFORE ME, AND TELL THE GUARD THAT YOU HAVE AN ERRAND TO RUN AT A NUNNERY ON THE SOUTH SIDE OF THE KYICHU RIVER.

WHAT ABOUT YOU, KUNDUN?

I'LL MAKE MY ESCAPE TONIGHT. WE'LL MEET UP AGAIN LATER ON.

I'M SURE THERE ARE SPIES WORKING FOR THE CHINESE AMONG THE CROWD...

PLEASE KEEP OUR PLAN ABSOLUTELY CONFIDENTIAL UNTIL WE'VE LEFT LHASA COMPLETELY.

AND ONCE WE'VE CONFIRMED OUR ESCAPE, PLEASE LET THE CROWD KNOW ABOUT IT, AND REQUEST THAT THEY LEAVE IMMEDIATELY.

I MUST PROTECT THE LIVES OF LHASA CITIZENS. I TRUST YOUR LEADERSHIP, AND BEG YOU FOR YOUR COOPERATION.

MAHAKALA, MY PERSONAL PROTECTOR DIVINITY... I AM HERE TO SAY GOOD-BYE...

EVERY ONE OF YOU HAVE BEEN PRAYING FOR MY SAFE JOURNEY...

THANK YOU...

IT MAY TAKE A WHILE...

BUT I WILL COME BACK... I PROMISE....

WE'VE MANAGED TO GET THROUGH THE CROWD.

NOW, THE CHINESE SOLDIERS ARE AHEAD OF US.

PLEASE WATCH YOUR STEP. WE'RE CROSSING THE RIVER-BANK.

TICK

IF THEY CATCH US HERE, ALL OUR EFFORTS WILL HAVE BEEN IN VAIN, AND COUNTLESS LIVES WILL BE LOST...

WE MUST GET OUT OF HERE IN ONE PIECE...

THE JOURNEY CONTINUES BY BOAT FROM HERE!

WE'VE BEEN WAITING FOR YOU, YOUR HOLINESS!

OH! TIBETAN FREEDOM FIGHTERS!

ALLOW US TO ESCORT YOU FROM HERE!

YOU'RE IN GOOD HANDS.

WE JUST CAUGHT UP WITH THE PRECEDING PARTY.

OK, LET'S KEEP GOING!

WHAT A RELIEF! MY MOM AND TENDZIN ARE FINE!

ALL RIGHT!

WE'RE HEADING TOWARDS CHE-LA MOUNTAIN PASS.

PLEASE LET ME KNOW WHEN YOU'RE TIRED.

WE'LL BE ARRIVING SOON AT A SMALL VILLAGE. LET'S TAKE A SHORT BREAK THERE.

DO YOU KNOW WHAT THE CHINESE ARMY IS DOING?

IF THEY FIGURE OUT WHERE WE ARE, THEY'LL BE ABLE TO PREDICT OUR DESIRED ROUTE AND AMBUSH US ALONG THE WAY.

WE HAVE TO HURRY UP!

IS IT REALLY ALL RIGHT YOUR HOLINESS? WE'RE EMBARRASSED TO OFFER YOU SUCH SHABBY ACCOMMODATIONS.

DON'T BE. WE'RE THANKFUL FOR YOUR HOSPITALITY.

ARE YOU ALL RIGHT, MOTHER...?

DON'T WORRY!

HOW ARE YOU DOING, YOUR HOLINESS?

I'M DOING WELL... BUT I'M CONCERNED ABOUT THE ELDERS...

EVERYONE, PLEASE KEEP YOUR SPIRITS UP! WE HAVE TO KEEP GOING AND GET FURTHER AWAY FROM THIS AREA BEFORE THE STATIONARY TROOPS FIND US.

THUBALUP
THUBALUP

WHAT!?

YOUR HOLINESS... WE RECEIVED SOME BAD NEWS...

WHAT IS IT?

WELL... 48 HOURS AFTER YOUR EVACUATION FROM NORBULINGKA...

THE CHINESE ARMY SHELLED THE PALACE!

THEY EVEN FIRED ON THE INNOCENT CROWD STANDING NEARBY...

AND THE FIRE HAS LASTED FOR 41 HOURS...

KABOOM!

BAAADOOOW

TWO WEEKS SINCE THE ESCAPE, ARRIVAL IN *LHUNTSE DZONG*, A BORDER TOWN AT THE INDIAN BORDER

WE HAVE NO TOLERANCE FOR THE INHUMANE ACTS AND BRUTAL CRIMES COMMITTED BY THE CHINESE!

WE HEREBY OFFICIALLY REJECT THE SEVENTEEN-POINT AGREEMENT!

AT THE SAME TIME, I WISH TO CONFIRM THE RE-ESTABLISHMENT OF THE TIBETAN GOVERNMENT AS THE NATION'S SOLE ADMINISTRATIVE BODY.

THE NEW GOVERNMENT WILL SEEK ASYLUM IN INDIA, AND WILL TRY TO OPEN NEGOTIATIONS WITH THE CHINESE FROM THERE!

YEH!

YEH!

YEH!!

YOUR HOLINESS, GET TO INDIA AS SOON AS POSSIBLE!

THE CHINESE ARMY IS RIGHT BEHIND US!!

WHAT
HAPPENED,
YOUR
HOLINESS!?

KUNDUN!!

IT'S LUCKY THAT
WE FOUND THIS SHACK,
BUT HE HAS SUCH
A HIGH FEVER...

HE MUST
HAVE
DYSENTERY...

WHAT SHOULD
WE DO?
FOR THE TIME
BEING, SHOULD
WE STAY PUT?

I THINK HE'S TOO
ILL TO GO ON...

NO,
I INSIST!
WE MUST
MOVE ON!

YOUR
HOLINESS!

PANCHEN LAMA... I'M WORRIED ABOUT YOU. I WONDER HOW THINGS ARE FOR YOU NOW...

YOUR HOLINESS... WE HAVE ARRIVED AT THE BORDER.

BORDER POST NA/102

IT'S TIME TO SAY GOOD-BYE, ... KUNDUN.

BORDER POST NA/102

10. LEFT
H.H. The Dalai Lama attending
the 2500th Buddha Jayanti
Anniversary in 1956

11. BELOW
Debating with the most
outstanding scholars
of three major monasteries at
the Geshe final examination.

Source:
Tibet Religious Foundation of His Holiness the Dalai Lama

12. ABOVE
The Lhasa uprising
on March 11, 1959

13. BELOW
Chinese tank troops arriving
in Lhasa on March 20, 1959

Source:
Tibet Religious Foundation of
His Holiness the Dalai Lama

14. ABOVE
En route to exile in India

15. BELOW
H.H. The Dalai Lama and his younger brother,
Tendzin Choegyal, en route to exile in India

Source:
Tibet Religious Foundation of His Holiness the Dalai Lama

CHAIRMAN MAO! ALLOW ME TO REPORT TO YOU!

ORDER IN LHASA HAS BEEN COMPLETELY RESTORED.

I SEE... BUT WHAT HAS HAPPENED TO THE DALAI LAMA?

WELL... UNFORTUNATELY, WE LOST TRACK OF HIM!

I'M AFRAID HE FLED ABROAD...

.....

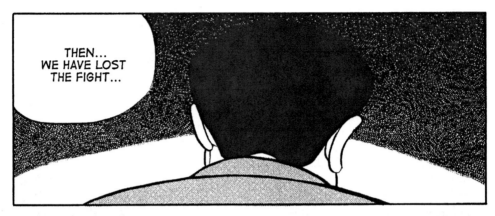

THEN...
WE HAVE LOST
THE FIGHT...

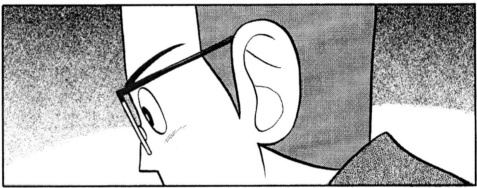

APRIL, 1959
ARRIVAL IN THE INDIAN TOWN
OF MUSSOORIE

KUNDUN,
HOW ARE YOU
FEELING NOW?

THANK YOU,
MOTHER. I
FEEL MUCH
BETTER.

I READ THE WELCOME MESSAGE ON THE TELEGRAM FROM INDIAN PRIME MINISTER *NEHRU*.

HE TOLD ME THAT HE WOULD DO EVERYTHING HE COULD TO ACCOMMODATE US IN INDIA.

THAT'S WONDERFUL NEWS... OF COURSE, WE STILL HAVE A LOT OF ISSUES TO SORT OUT...

MOTHER... YOU MIGHT SOMETIMES WONDER WHY YOUR SON BECAME THE DALAI LAMA...

INDEED, THERE ARE SO MANY PROBLEMS AHEAD OF US... AND I FEEL... I AM HERE IN ORDER TO FACE THIS CHALLENGE.

THE CHINESE AUTHORITIES CONTINUED ARRESTING ANYONE WHO WAS DIRECTLY OR INDIRECTLY INVOLVED IN PROTESTS.

THESE PEOPLE WERE NOT ONLY IMPRISONED, BUT ALSO SENT TO CONCENTRATION CAMPS TO DO FORCED LABOR OR FORCED TO STUDY COMMUNISM. MANY WERE MURDERED OUTRIGHT...

I DO SEE THAT ANGER AND HATRED CAN GROW INSIDE AND CLOUD PEOPLE'S VISION...

LORD BUDDHA... NOW MORE THAN EVER IT IS TIME FOR ME TO EMBRACE YOUR PRECIOUS TEACHINGS...

I WILL CHERISH BEINGS OF BAD NATURE, AND THOSE OPPRESSED BY STRONG SINS AND SUFFERINGS, AS IF I HAD FOUND A PRECIOUS TREASURE VERY DIFFICULT TO FIND.

A REFUGEE CAMP IN INDIA

YOUR HOLINESS!!

KUNDUN!

WE WERE LUCKY TO GET HERE ALIVE!

SO MANY FROZE OR STARVED TO DEATH ON THE WAY THROUGH THE MOUNTAINS!!

I FEEL YOUR PAIN, BUT PLEASE DON'T LOSE HOPE!

LET'S KEEP OUR SPIRITS UP! AND SOMEDAY SOON WE WILL GO BACK TO TIBET TOGETHER!!

YOUR HOLINESS, THE NUMBER OF TIBETAN REFUGEES IS INCREASING DRAMATICALLY...

PANCHEN LAMA!!

MARCH 1964
AT THE MONLAM GREAT PRAYER FESTIVAL

LADIES AND GENTLEMEN...
DALAI LAMA IS...
THE REAL...
DALAI LAMA IS...

RIGHT ON!
GO AHEAD...
RIP THE DALAI LAMA
TO SHREDS!!

I KNOW
THE DALAI LAMA
PERSONALLY...
WHO HE
REALLY IS...

LISTEN,
EVERYONE!
DALAI LAMA
IS THE REAL
LEADER OF
TIBET!!

TIBET'S FREEDOM WILL
BE REGAINED SOMEDAY,
AND HE'LL BE BACK ON
THE THRONE FOR US!!

YEAH!

GOHOO!

YAAAAY!

AND EVERYONE HAS A RIGHT TO SEE THESE WISHES COME TRUE.

LONG LIVE THE INDEPENDENCE OF TIBET!!

WE PROHIBIT YOU FROM GOING OUTSIDE AT NIGHT!

IF YOU VIOLATE THE CURFEW, WE WILL HAVE TO KILL YOU!!

IN THE MIDST OF OUR STRUGGLES, I BELIEVE THAT WHAT KEEPS US GOING IS... **HOPE.**

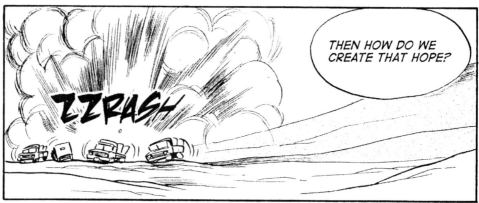

ZZRASH

THEN HOW DO WE CREATE THAT HOPE?

THERE WAS A TIBETAN REBEL GROUP BASED IN NORTHERN NEPAL...

THEY USED TO ENGAGE IN ARMED FIGHTING WITH THE CHINESE LIBERATION ARMY.

ONE TIME, WITH A LOT OF SUPPORT FROM THE CIA, THESE REBELS WERE ABLE TO WIPE OUT ENTIRE CONVOYS OF CHINESE TROOPS.

BUT I ASK YOU... CAN THIS HOPE THAT INSPIRES US POSSIBLY STEM FROM ARMED BATTLES?

BLAM

I DO NOT THINK SO. THEIR SMALL, TEMPORARY VICTORY GAVE THE CHINESE A CONVENIENT PRETEXT TO ATTACK TIBET WITH EVEN STRONGER FORCE.

AS OF 1979, MORE THAN 1.2 MILLION TIBETAN LIVES HAVE BEEN LOST, AND THIS NUMBER IS INCREASING EACH DAY.

AS MANY AS 5125 TEMPLES AND MONASTERIES HAVE BEEN DESTROYED.

BA-DOOOM

ANYWHERE ELSE ON THIS PLANET... NO MATTER HOW FURIOUS AND AGGRESSIVE WE BECOME, IT WILL ALWAYS BE IMPOSSIBLE TO ERADICATE ALL OUR ENEMIES.

AS LONG AS WE KEEP OUR INTERNAL PREDATORS INSIDE OUR MINDS, ANGER AND HATRED, DESTROYING TODAY'S EXTERNAL PREDATORS DOES NOT MEAN MUCH...

BECAUSE TOMORROW YOU WILL HAVE MORE PREDATORS.

HOPE CANNOT BE BORN FROM ANGER OR VIOLENCE.

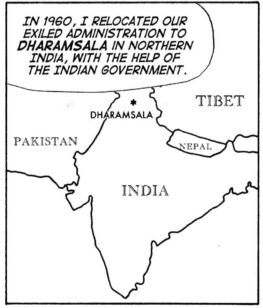

IN 1960, I RELOCATED OUR EXILED ADMINISTRATION TO **DHARAMSALA** IN NORTHERN INDIA, WITH THE HELP OF THE INDIAN GOVERNMENT.

TIBET

DHARAMSALA

PAKISTAN

NEPAL

INDIA

THE FIRST THING WE DID IN THIS NEW FRONTIER WAS BUILD ORPHANAGES, GIVING SHELTER AND EDUCATION TO THE INCREASING NUMBERS OF PARENTLESS CHILDREN.

WE ARE GRATEFUL TO THE INDIAN GOVERNMENT, WHICH ACCEPTED US AND SUPPLIED THE MAJORITY OF FUNDS FOR THESE FACILITIES.

CHILDREN ARE OUR MOST PRECIOUS TREASURE. IF WELL-INFORMED AND EDUCATED, THEY CAN PRESERVE TIBETAN CULTURE AND FURTHER DEVELOP IT FOR A HOPEFUL FUTURE.

TODAY, MORE THAN 140,000 TIBETANS LIVE IN EXILE.

IN UNFAMILIAR LIVING CONDITIONS IN FOREIGN LANDS, THESE PEOPLE HAVE WORKED HARD, PATIENTLY FOSTERING THEIR HOPE WITH SUPPORT FROM THE INDIAN PEOPLE, AND ON A LARGER SCALE, FROM THE GLOBAL COMMUNITY, AS WELL.

NOW, DHARAMSALA IS AFFECTIONATELY KNOWN AS "LITTLE LHASA", AND HAS DEVELOPED INTO A PROSPEROUS TOWN AS A TIBETAN COMMUNITY.

WE HAVE BEEN ABLE TO REBUILD SOME TEMPLES IN DHARAMSALA.

SOME OF OUR TRADITIONAL FESTIVALS AND IMPORTANT RITUALS WERE REVIVED AND ARE ONCE AGAIN HELD IN THESE TEMPLES, IN ACCORDANCE WITH OUR TRADITIONAL TIBETAN CALENDAR.

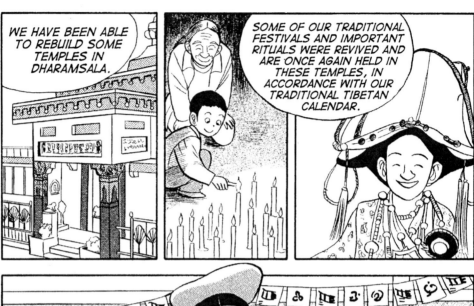

SOME WONDER WHY WE HAVE BEEN ABLE TO MAINTAIN SUCH RESILIENCE AND OPTIMISM.

OTHERS WONDER WHY WE HAVE BEEN ABLE TO STAND FIRM WITHOUT THE NEED FOR ARMED FORCES OVER THE PAST FEW DECADES.

IT'S BECAUSE WE HAVE RECEIVED SO MUCH **LOVE** AND **COMPASSION** FROM PEOPLE ALL AROUND THE WORLD.

LOVE AND COMPASSION FOSTER HOPE.

I LOST MY FREEDOM AT THE AGE OF 15.

I LOST MY COUNTRY AT THE AGE OF 24.

FOR THE LAST 50 YEARS, I HAVE BEEN IN EXILE, FULFILLING AN IMPORTANT RESPONSIBILITY.

THAT IS TO REGAIN THE COMPREHENSIVE AUTONOMY OF TIBET.

2008

DALAI LAMA, 73 YEARS OLD

I THANK YOU FOR YOUR INVITATION FROM ABROAD AND FOR THIS OPPORTUNITY TO SHARE WITH YOU TODAY THE STORIES ABOUT TIBET.

I HAVE RECEIVED SO MUCH SUPPORT FROM SO MANY PEOPLE OF SO MANY DIFFERENT BACKGROUNDS...

EVEN FROM HOLLYWOOD...

AND FROM OTHER SPIRITUAL LEADERS...

I AM ALWAYS TOUCHED BY THE LOVE AND COMPASSION OF THESE PEOPLE...

IT MAY SOUND STRANGE TO YOU...

BUT NOW I WOULD LIKE TO EXTEND THAT PRECIOUS GIFT TO OUR CHINESE BROTHERS AND SISTERS.

MANY YOUNG, AMBITIOUS STUDENTS AND ACTIVISTS LOST THEIR LIVES IN THE **TIANANMEN SQUARE MASSACRE.**

LIVE DIE

BRRRRRR

MY HEART GOES OUT TO ALL OF THE VICTIMS WHO WERE SEEKING A **DEMOCRACY** AND A TRULY JUST SOCIETY, WHERE COMPASSION AND LOVE PLAY IMPERATIVE ROLES.

DESPITE PHENOMENAL ECONOMIC GROWTH, I FEEL THAT CHINA HAS LOST SPIRITUAL WEALTH.

I VERY MUCH HOPE THAT SOMEDAY CHINA WILL REGAIN THESE VIRTUES, AND BECOME A TRULY "WEALTHY" COUNTRY.

THEY TOO GO THROUGH A DIFFERENT KIND OF SUFFERING. AND I THINK WE, TIBETANS, HAVE SOMETHING TO GIVE.

TODAY THE WORLD IS SO INTERDEPENDENT. ACTING WITH COMPASSION TO OTHERS WILL ULTIMATELY BENEFIT YOUR OWN WELLBEING.

WE, HUMAN BEINGS, HAVE AN INBORN GIFT TO LOVE AND CARE ABOUT OTHERS.

NO COMPLICATED DOGMA OR RELIGIOUS TEACHINGS ARE NECESSARY TO BE ABLE TO LOVE.

OUR OWN HEART IS OUR TEMPLE. OUR KINDNESS IS OUR DOGMA.

AND OUR COMPASSION WILL LEAD THE WORLD TOWARDS PEACE, GENERATING HOPE FOR HAPPINESS.

WHERE ARE YOUR PARENTS, YOUNG BOY?

THEY WERE SHOT TO DEATH DURING THE TRIP. I AM THE ONLY ONE WHO SURVIVED...

BAAAANG

BAAANG

RUN, RUN!

DON'T LOOK BACK! RUN!!

WOULD YOU FIND A ROOM FOR HIM?

YES, YOUR HOLINESS.

IT WILL BE ALL RIGHT, LITTLE ONE. REST WELL.

I WILL TELL YOU WHAT... I AM PLANNING TO TRANSFORM OUR BEAUTIFUL TIBETAN PLATEAU INTO THE WORLD'S LARGEST NATURAL PARK.

IS THAT TRUE?

YES, IT'S TRUE.

FOR AS LONG AS
SPACE ENDURES,
AND FOR AS LONG AS
LIVING BEINGS REMAIN,
UNTIL THEN
MAY I, TOO, ABIDE
TO DISPEL THE MISERY
OF THE WORLD.

~~ THE END ~~

16. ABOVE
H.H. The Dalai Lama
and his mother,
Dekyi Tsering

17. RIGHT
Receiving the first group
of Tibetan refugee children

Source:
Tibet Religious Foundation
of His Holiness the Dalai Lama

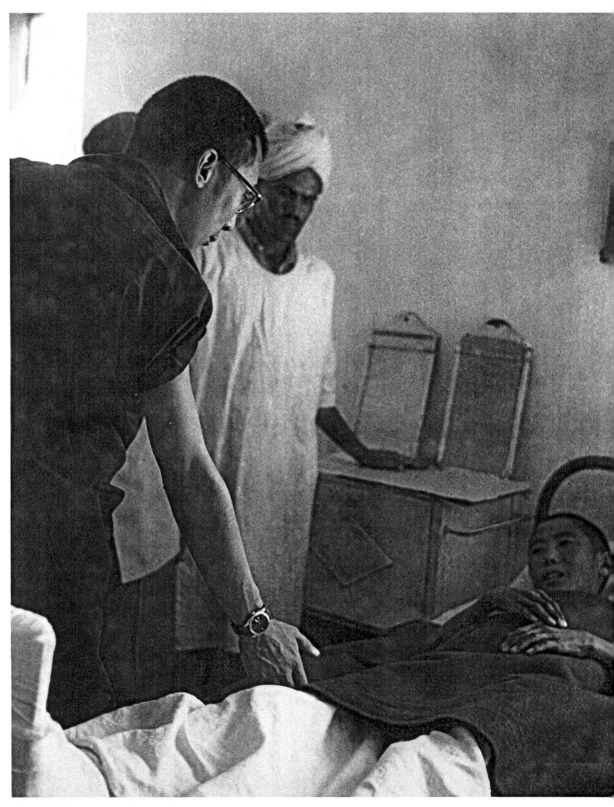

18. ABOVE
H.H. The Dalai Lama consoling the patients in the community hospital

Source: Tibet Religious Foundation
His Holiness the Dalai Lama

9. ABOVE
Watching the monks in debate

20. BELOW
Being moved to tears by the benevolence of Buddha and Bodhisattva

Source: Tibet Religious Foundation of His Holiness the Dalai Lama 211

21. ABOVE
With former US President Bill Clinton
and former US Vice-President Al Gore

22. BELOW
Pleasant talks with
His Holiness Pope John Paul II

3. ABOVE
raying with Islamic leaders

24. BELOW
Bending down to light the lamps in front of the Hindu statue

Source: Tibet Religious Foundation of His Holiness the Dalai Lama

213

25. ABOVE LEFT
With former South African
President, Nelson Mandela

26. ABOVE RIGHT
With Mother Teresa

27. RIGHT
Receiving the Nobel Prize
for Peace in 1989

EPILOGUE

OSLO, NORWAY 1989,
UPON RECEIVING THE NOBEL PRIZE FOR PEACE

DALAI LAMA ADDRESSED THE AUDIENCE...

INDIVIDUALLY, THIS PRIZE DOES NOT MEAN MUCH TO ME.

HOWEVER, FOR THE ENTIRE TIBETAN POPULATION, IT MEANS SO MUCH.

THE TRUE RECIPIENT OF THIS PRIZE FOR PEACE IS NO OTHER THAN THE TIBETAN PEOPLE.

TIBETAN PEOPLE HAVE WITNESSED THE DESTRUCTION OF THEIR SPIRITUAL SITES AND THE DESTRUCTION OF THEIR NATURAL RESOURCES UNDER AGGRESSIVE DEVELOPMENT PLANS.

THE WHOLE ECO-SYSTEM WAS DESTROYED... HERDS OF DRONGS, TIBETAN SEROWS, AND OTHER WILD ANIMALS ARE NO LONGER IN SIGHT.

IN ADDITION, CONTAINING MORE *URANIUM* IN THEIR SOIL THAN OTHER COUNTRIES, TIBET HAS BECOME A MAJOR MINING RESOURCE, AND AS A RESULT, FACES SERIOUS RADIOACTIVE CONTAMINATION.

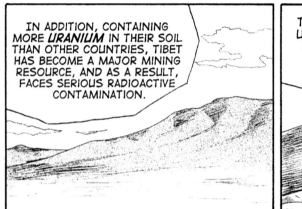

THEIR LAND IS ALSO BEING USED FOR PRODUCTION OF NUCLEAR WEAPONS, AND FOR THE DISPOSAL OF *NUCLEAR WASTE*...

THE OPENING OF THE *QINGZANG RAILWAY* HAS DIRECTLY CONNECTED MAJOR CHINESE CITIES TO LHASA. THE CHINESE GOVERNMENT ENCOURAGES A LARGE NUMBER OF CHINESE PEOPLE TO FLOOD INTO TIBET TO SETTLE THERE.

MORE THAN 7 MILLION CHINESE HAVE SETTLED IN TIBET, WHOSE POPULATION IS 6 MILLION. THE NUMBER OF CHINESE IN TIBET IS EXPECTED TO GROW TO APPROXIMATELY 20 MILLION BEFORE LONG WHILE "*SINICIZATION*" OF TIBETAN PEOPLE IS UNDERWAY.

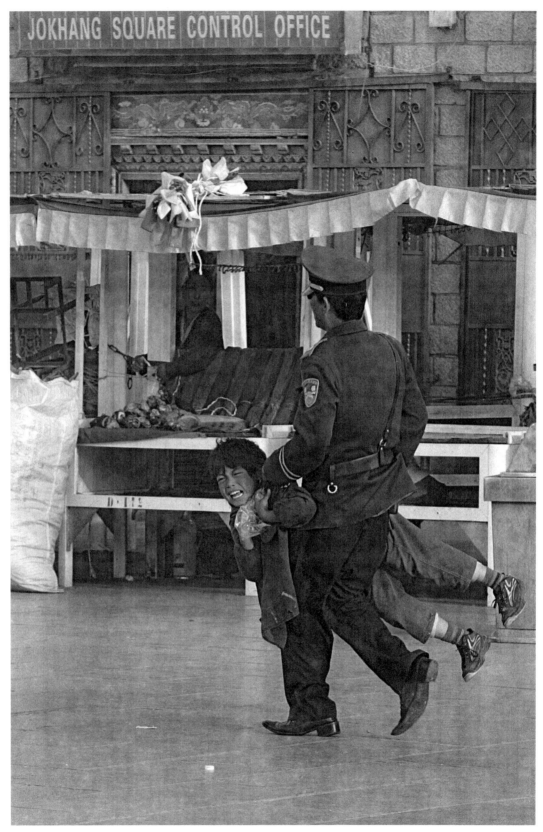

28. ABOVE
Chinese security at the Jokhang Square, Lhasa in 2005

Source: Copyright© 2005 by Pedro Saraiva

29. ABOVE
Old Tibetan man looking at a photograph
of the Dalai Lama at the Drepung Monastery

Source: Copyright© 1986 by Gert Holmertz

END NOTE

In reference to the Tiananmen Massacre which took place in 1989, His Holiness the Dalai Lama made the following comment.

"Millions of Chinese brothers and sisters displayed openly and peacefully their yearning for freedom, democracy and human dignity... they embraced non-violence in a most impressive way reflecting the values for which the movement stood... I believe strongly that the international community has an obligation to morally and politically support the Chinese democracy movement. China needs human rights, democracy and the rule of law. These values are the foundation of a free, dynamic, stable and peaceful society... Therefore, every effort should be made to bring China also into the mainstream of the world democracy."

To me, his comments were an embodiment of his Non-violence doctrine, and made me realize again and again the depth of what his words stand for.

It was more than two years ago that Mr. Eiji Han Shimizu of Emotional Content brought me the idea to graphically adapt the life of His Holiness the Dalai Lama and the historical events of Tibet. Since then, I have faced the notion of "Non-violence" everyday, and realized that the doctrine is not a mere absence of violence, but a relentless effort to create an agreeable understanding even between enemies, and a greater solidarity regarding the issue at stake among people around the world. I believe that such proactive attitudes will foster hope for the future, and change the world for the better in the long run.

In anticipation for the Beijing Olympics in 2008, many angry protesters attacked the Olympic torch runners in an effort to undermine the pride of China and its people. In the final inking process of my work, I witnessed this with great sadness as these acts of protest inflicted more anger and hatred on both sides, and that some Free Tibet Movements were drifting further away from the doctrine of Non-violence that His Holiness advocates.

Tibet was invaded and occupied by the Chinese under the name of emancipation from foreign occupation forces. The world has committed so many wartime atrocities, including my own country in the last century using the same pretext. Even at this moment, we are witnessing more and more miseries and tragedies being created.

Manga is an incredibly powerful and effective storytelling vehicle, and I hope that my work helps to spread the Non-violence doctrine further as a solution to all these conflicts.

Tetsu Saiwai
Wakayama, Japan
June, 2008

ACKNOWLEDGEMENT

This work would have not been possible without the kind contributions from
The Liaison Office of His Holiness the Dalai Lama for Japan and East Asia.
The publisher would like to particularly thank Mr. Chope Paljor Tsering,
former representative of the liaison office, for attaining authorization from
the Government of Tibet in Exile in Dharamsala; and Mr. Lhakpa Tshoko,
current representative of the liaison office, for his insightful advice and
for coordinating the photo archive with their Taipei representative.

To support the exiled Tibetan community via the Liaison Office, please visit:
http://www.tibethouse.jp/support/index.html (Japanese)

The autobiography of His Holiness, "Freedom in Exile"
and "Kundun", a feature film directed by Mr. Martin Scorsese, became
an essential source of information and inspiration for our work.
We hope that our depiction of the Tibetan landscape, architecture, and
costume appear close to its reality.

We thank the Religious Foundation of His Holiness the Dalai Lama for
generously allowing us access to photo images which provided invaluable
richness and reality to our graphic novel.

We would also like to thank the photographers from around the world for
lending their talent and images to us. Thank you to Mr. Pedro Saraiva,
Mr. Gert Holmertz, and Mr. Stephan Bollinger for understanding the cause
of the project.

Lastly, we thank our friends and family members for their unwavering
inspiration and encouragement.

BIBLIOGRAPHY

Interviews

1. Tsering, Chope Paljor. Personal interview. Dec. 2006.

2. Tshoko, Lhakpa. Personal interview. Aug. 2007.

DVDs

1. Biography - Dalai Lama: the Soul of Tibet. DVD. A&E Home Video, 2005.

2. COMPASSION IN EXILE: the Story of the 14th Dali Lama. Dir. Mickey Lemle. DVD. 1992.

3. Dalai Lama on Life and Enlightenment. DVD. Hannover House, 2006.

4. Escape Over the Himalayas. Dir. Maria Blumencron. DVD. Tibet Support Group KIKU, 2006.

5. Kundun. Dir. Martin Scorsese. Perf. Tenzin Thuthob Tsarong. DVD. 1998.

Books

1. Gyalpo, Pema. Tibet Nyumon. Tokyo: Nicchu Shuppan, 1998.

2. Ishihama, Yumiko, and Kazuo Nagahashi. Zusetsu Tibet Rekishi Kikou. Tokyo: Kawade Shobo Shinsha, 1999.

3. Tenzin Gyatso, Dalai Lama, and Howard C. Cutler. The Art of Happiness: a Handbook for Living. New York: Riverhead Hardcover, 1998.

4. Tenzin Gyatso, Dalai Lama. Freedom in Exile: the Autobiography of the Dalai Lama. New York: HarperCollins, 199

5. Tenzin Gyatso, Dalai Lama. Idaku Kotoba. Tokyo: East P, 2006.

Websites

1. "Latest News." His Holiness the 14th Dalai Lama. The Office of His Holiness the Dalai Lama. Mar. 2006 <http://www.dalailama.com/>.

2. "Messages from His Holiness the Dalai Lama."LIAISON OFFICE OF H.H.THE DALAI LAMA for Japan & East-Asia LIAISON OFFICE OF H.H.THE DALAI LAMA for Japan & East-Asia. 20 May 2006 <http://www.tibethouse.jp/dalai_lama/message/index.html>.

3. "Present Situation in Tibet." Tibet Government in Exile's Official Web Site. The Government of Tibet in Exile. May 2008 <http://www.tibet.com/Humanrights/index.html>.

4. "Tenzin Gyatso, 14th Dalai Lama." Wikipedia the Free Encyclopedia. Wikimedia Foundation, Inc. Aug. 2006 <http://en.wikipedia.org/wiki/Tenzin_Gyatso>.

5. "Tibet in Exile." The Official Website of the Central Tibetan Administration. The Central Tibetan Administration. Aug. 2007 <http://www.tibet.net/en/tibet/exile.html>.

6. "Tibet News." International Campaign for Tibet. International Campaign for Tibet. June 2006 <http://www.savetibet.org/news/index.php>.

ABOUT THE AUTHOR

Tetsu Saiwai is a manga artist from Japan.

Throughout his career. spanning over twenty years, he has published
a number of educational mangas with regards to environmental protections
and human rights issues.

Aside from mangas, he is a passionate puppeteer, and plans to open
a puppet troupe to advocate similar and important themes for humanity.
Tetsu lives in the beautiful countryside of Western Japan with his wife and dogs.

To learn more about his works, visit:
http://blogs.yahoo.co.jp/saiwaimiyuki/folder/1587623.html (Japanese)

ABOUT EMOTIONAL CONTENT

Emotional Content is a network of independent Manga (Japanese term for
graphic novels or comic books) and Anime (animation in English) artists in Japan.

Our mission is to create and distribute media content that will INFORM, INSPIRE,
and EMPOWER others to generate positive actionsin the world.

Currently, a dozen Manga and one Anime project are under development, and
we hope to share these informative,inspirational, and empowering works with
you soon!

Please visit us for updates.
www.biographicnovel.com
www.emotionalcontent.net

Our business operation is based in Los Angeles, California, and our production
center is based in Yokohama, Japan.

Contact address:
Emotional Content LLC.
P.O. Box 251863
Los Angeles, CA 90025
info@biographicnovel.com

EMOTIONAL
CONTENT

Printed in the United States
135602LV00003B/20/P

9 780981 754307